REINVENTING AND REDEFINING YOU

HOW DO YOU CHOOSE TODAY'S SOCIAL MEDIA TOOLS TO OPTIMISE YOUR ONLINE AND OFFLINE PRESENCE?

DR. AMIT DAS

Made with ♥ on the Notion Press Platform
www.notionpress.com

To

All my bosses and mentors who made a difference in my professional career.

"A personal brand is a never-ending undertaking that develops and evolves. Your personal brand will be more engaging if you can add more color to your story. Reinventing oneself is essentially a process of self-transformation."

- Dr. Amit Das, Motivational Speaker, Leadership Coach , Counsellor, and Mentor.

Contents

Foreword

Dear Reader,

This book is for everyone who wants to make a good difference in their lives. Learn how to use individual branding if you want to have a successful career and achieve your goals. Before you can learn much about how to use individual branding for a concentrated advantage, you must first understand what individual branding is.

The authors detail how to select the top social media platforms today for your unique objectives, how to create an authentic storyline, how to appear in search results and then optimise your online presence, how to benefit from both online and offline networking to maximise both, and how to use your expertise to publish a book or give a public speech. Use the hottest social networking sites available today, including LinkedIn, Facebook, Instagram, Youtube and SnapChat. This book is filled with innovative methods and strategies that are doable, simple, and successful.

For more than two decades, the author of this book has worked in the fields of learning management and marketing. The most dynamic individuals are aware of what makes them unique, captivating, and distinct from the herd. Learn how to take advantage of these differences and use them to your advantage. Developing your own brand will provide you with a competitive advantage as well as the sought-after position of market leader! Everyone has a unique identity. Here, the author will provide you with some quick suggestions to help you stand out among your peers, network, and industry. To stand out and make a difference with your personal brand, the author will show you how to create a consistent action plan, connect rather than network, and manage your energy rather than your time.

This book is a step-by-step guide to help you assess your strengths, help you develop a compelling personal brand, and make sure that your coworkers and network recognise your value and the contributions you make, whether you want to change careers, find a new job, or get promoted at your current organisation. The author uses a combination of tales, and examples from well-known leaders to explain how you should approach your career objectives and live the life you really desire. You'll learn how to reinvent yourself in this book to get a new job and prove your value to your existing organisation.

This book will teach you how to develop a following market for your branding, and make money off of your influence, including how much to charge. Additionally, you'll discover how to land an agency, attract the attention of prestigious media outlets and websites, and highlight a brand without alienating its rivals. You'll discover how to improve your online presence, comprehend the social media guidelines for influencer marketing, and find out how to monetise your passions.

This book is the secret to developing an incredible brand for any entrepreneur, coach, or trainer. The author has eloquently articulated personal branding as a tool for helping people construct their own presence beyond their wildest dreams. He recognises that intelligent, motivated individuals like you have special gifts to give the world, but it's difficult to do in this competitive environment. The author has spent his entire professional career assisting managers in increasing their productivity, which he describes as the capacity to make progress on the results that matter most to them professionally and individually.

This book is a career-changing book written by an experienced mentor and motivational speaker. It'll give your mind a makeover, reshaping your perceptions and reframing your most established beliefs into new, positive, practical steps to help you develop a great personal brand. Become the go-to guru for anything you do by attracting the proper relationships and attention. In every organisation, industry, or profession, the highest paid employees are not always the most qualified, gifted, or best. They're the most well-known. They are well-liked, respected, recommended, employed, and introduced. With practical insight and strategic counsel for establishing your personal brand, this book provides you with the inside route to the top. If you create a distinct and trustworthy brand for your company, it will most certainly be more successful on the internet.

The author goes right to the point about how to accomplish it, and they back it up with examples to help you engage your audience and solve problems. Through his profession, he's seen that the vast majority of time management advice offered doesn't help you enhance your life. He leads his reader through a thorough combination of his life experiences and coaching method in this bookresulting in a lot of clarity around the notion of personal branding. He explores many notions of personal branding, as well as why such branding "you" is necessary in today's competitive world.

This book attempts to provide insights into the many pathways, courses, and drives that world-class enterprises have constructed in order to achieve the pinnacles of greatness. This book provides cutting-edge material, including innovative and unusual study aids as well as fresh, thought-provoking content. It reveals numerous methods for intentionally cultivating a mindset that refuses to be superficial about life. This book will appeal to practitioners who want to increase their personal effectiveness in social media. The author demonstrates how to uncover your hidden talent, transform ideals into actions, and open up communication across audiences.

If you're seeking a means to build yourself as most recognisable brand, look no further. You can now choose. Clicking the order button now can either transform your life for the better or worse for the foreseeable future compared to doing nothing. In order to position yourself as one of the top candidates for your desired position, grow in your career, and secure the business opportunities you're chasing, learn how to refocus your skills and expertise in this book. The objective of this book is to assist you in changing the manner in which you communicate who you are, what you actually do, and the distinctive value that you offer to others and your clients. Here, the author of this book breaks down the essential components of impactful stories, which will inspire you to think further.

As the author demonstrates in this book, by building your personality, you can increase communication, raise morale, encourage trust, and keep negativity at bay within yourselves. The author of this book, has a unique combination of expertise and insight, having worked as a management consultant. His insights and interviews from business sectors are used to demonstrate the obstacles to high brand value and brand leadership. The author has chosen a straightforward, customised, and compelling approach to the subject of personal branding in this book. He combines a delicate fusion of his own tales with a timeless viewpoint on one's duty as an industry brand representative. He has developed an everlasting presence that attracts his clients effortlessly after overcoming the challenge of figuring out how to build his business and obtain new clients effortlessly.

If you're a recent graduate, a seasoned professional, a freelancer, an entrepreneur, or simply someone who wants to start building their personal brand online in a methodical fashion, this book is for you. So brand yourself first for the role you want, and your career or business will soar to new heights.

Once again, thank you for taking the time to learn more about how do you choose today's social media tools to optimise your online and offline presence? Thank you for taking the time to read this book. Once you've converted your social networking accounts to business accounts, you may start making money with them. You'll discover all you need to know about the marketing budget you'll need to succeed, as well as the many strategies you may employ to attract your target audience. The solution to this is to create and maintain your personal brand.

Carpe diem.
Dr. Amit Das
Leadership Coach , Counsellor, and Mentor.

Preface

"Your brand is the single most important investment you can create it for yourself"

What justifies reading this book?

The art of personal branding involves how you present yourself to others so they will remember you. In today's digital world, it's critical to develop and maintain your personal brand. Learn from some of the top personal branding tricks from this book. You'll learn about your profession and yourself in this book. I will begins with a recent 2022 story of a successful person who was able to brand himself despite all the challenges in his earlier life.

This booksheds light on what many perceive to be the art and science of branding and marketing, as well as its application to personal branding. Millions of marketers across the world utilise the tools and procedures detailed in the book to grow the brands they manage on a daily basis. If you can use these tried-and-true strategies to actually set yourself apart, it can be nothing short of spectacular.

No one can dream for you, no one can believe in you, and no one can assist you in reaching your objectives. So, what do you have to lose? This book outlines the importance of personal branding, clearing your head of clutter, and sticking to a single-point agenda. I would offer the most effective tactics and step-by-step instructions for you to construct your own particular road to excellence in this book. You'll also find better methods to collaborate with colleagues, respond more effectively to coaching and mentoring, and become more positive and self-directed in your thoughts and actions, resulting in more personal and professional pleasure.

You can review your online reputation what is very crucial, so learn how to Google yourself appropriately, produce, curate, and distribute information, and establish yourself as a thought leader in your field. You'll have the step-by-step instructions you need to start standing out from the competition, stand out in a global talent pool, and successfully establish a professional presence with a clear and concise image and reputation, whether you're looking for a new job, thinking about a career change, or want to be more successful in your career. The book gives you the vital knowledge, advice, and methods you need to build your own brand effectively.

Today, how well you're recognised determines your level of influence, which gives you an advantage in our environment. This book demonstrates its value in a straightforward and kind manner. Being successful entails more than just providing good at what you do; it also entails being the answer to people's problems, which leads them to select you over the competition. This book will assist you in thinking outside your comfort zone's invisible border and moving in the direction of clarity. This book gives you a taste of how I work with knowledge-givers and leaders to help them develop their presence. Writing this book has allowed me to pour my own personality into personal branding. It took me a long time to compile all of my tales and create something that is both personalised and helpful, but it was a worthwhile process that allowed me to really think about how I wanted to approach it.

By following my method, you may understand the universal narrative themes that all people respond to, the reasons why people buy things, how to develop a straightforward brand strategy, and how to develop persuasive messaging for your digital presence. This book is a how-to manual for using your differentiators to have more fruitful interactions. You'll learn how to become an influencer in this book. According to me, when they first started out, all of your favourite influencers had no followers.

The main goal of this book is to investigate the theme of personal branding, which is the process of creating and managing a personal brand based on an individual's essence—your values, beliefs, and life purpose—with the goal of making your personal brand strong, authentic, reliable, and highly differentiated.

A personal brand communicates a great deal about who you are and how you do business. It expresses your deeply held convictions and ideals. It shows your integrity to coworkers, employees, business partners, and customers.

I will provide you helpful advice on developing and sustaining a personal brand throughout your career. Your personal brand should be representative and coincide with your likes and hobbies. What do you wish to do, and which characteristics and qualities reflect your enthusiasm? If you want to be a professional speaker, market yourself as someone with public speaking abilities and ambition in your field of expertise. Create accounts on social networking sites that represent your interests. It's critical to optimise your LinkedIn profile to reflect your interests, talents, and goals. If you use Facebook and Twitter, make sure your profile and the information you provide on those platforms are consistent with your personal brand's overall tone and message. What are your plans for your own brand? You should construct a development path for yourself that leverages and buoys your personal brand, just as any commercial or corporate brand does.

You'll learn from this book that a personal brand is more than simply a CV, resume, and business card. Learn how to use the tried-and-true techniques of conventional personal branding to grow your brand through social media, online forums, and digital job boards. This book aims to teach you how critical it is to be productive every day toward achieving the things that matter most to you, leaving no stone unturned, and to develop a mindset of seeing the most overlooked aspects of life not only for what they are or appear to be, but also for what they could be. This book is a quest to perceive even the most mundane things in a new light. Its goal is to assist you to harness your capacity to become more productive and use it to your advantage in order to rise above the mediocre tides in all aspects of your life.

Whether you're just starting out or a seasoned entrepreneur or information provider, if you want to truly grasp the notion of standing out in business while still being your beautiful self, this book will guide you step by step toward effectively building your presence. Through the chapters in this book, you may spark your own genius and unearth all of your skills that have been latent for ages. The reader about the notion while also coaching them with thought-provoking questions that are basic yet effective in the process of developing one's presence. Each chapter is eye-opening and requires thought at every turn.

Regardless of the audience or venue, reading this book puts the reader on a unique and advantageous platform to connect in a more intelligent and successful manner. This book is well-researched and educational for people of all ages and genders. This book will teach you all you need to know about branding, including the ins and outs of social media, platforms, and tools for efficient content marketing. You will also acquire excellent content writing strategies in this book, which will assist you in a variety of ways when branding. After reading this book, you will be more familiar with numerous social media laws and the strategy of creating a good post for your social media accounts.

Every individual on the planet relies on word of mouth to influence their purchasing decisions, but less than 1% of businesses actively promote positive word of mouth.

I will talk about how to master brand building techniques so you can construct a powerful profile and a fearsome name. You'll learn how to recognise your brand and where it fits into the bigger picture, and then how to become the obvious option for whatever you do. Making a name for yourself isn't a question of chance or luck; it's a set of highly coachable talents that everyone can master. Learn how to establish a reputation, network with the right people, and publicise your accomplishments. Identify and develop your own brand, then strategically position yourself for maximum effect.

- Do you know what others are saying, both online and offline, about your personal brand?
- Are you making efforts to strengthen, hone, and improve it?
- Are you creating and enhancing your personal brand while promoting yourself in everything you do?

This bookcommunicates who you are, what you stand for, and why you are needed by future employers and similar partnerships. The beauty of the branding process is that after you've figured out who you are and what you really want, you'll intuitively know what kinds of professions, companies, and organisations you'd be a good fit for. This book will teach you how to create and maintain a unique personal brand creation approach that will help you improve your image by effectively packaging yourself for employers, contacts, and anyone who might be interested in who you are. It's all about self-packaging in your own branding scripts. It encapsulates the personal and professional attributes that businesses look for in new hires.

The book draws on first-hand experience from high-performance operations to deliver vital personal branding lessons as well as clear, accessible, and practical insights on building self-image in any corporate setting. This book provides a new and fascinating viewpoint on the factors that influence your millions of followers. Many entrepreneurs and knowledge-givers will find this book helpful in establishing and constructing a lucrative, impactful, and forceful presence.

This book discusses how to create and manage your personal brand by opening doors to opportunities, resources, and information. It will allow you to reclaim your capacity to form positive connections and form powerful networks. The book also goes into how to exhibit your unique style through clothing, communication, body language, and self-assurance. This book gives ideas and practical strategies for having a voice and making those favorable first impressions. Today, anyone can become an influencer, experiencing the best life has to offer while still making money. In reality, "Reinventing And Redefining You" will teach you how to accomplish just that. You'll learn how to use social media to establish your own brand, locate your target audience, create an excellent blog, and generate money by just posting a few times a day! Whether you currently have a large account with a lot of followers or have never made a single dime online, this book will take you by the hand and show you how to develop your brand from the ground up, gain adoring fans, and generate money effortlessly and consistently.

Effective personal branding will set you apart from the competition and help you acquire the trust of potential clients and employers. You only get one chance to create a first impression, so make it one that will set you apart from the competition. You are one-of-a-kind, and this bookenables you to identify and prioritise your distinctive abilities, skills, and interests in order to build your personal brand for the position you desire in your profession or business. This book will show you how to create, launch, monetise, and scale your own brand. It includes personal branding stories that will help you achieve your vision, mission, and goals in a focused manner.

It involves recognising a person's distinctive talents, marketable abilities, education, experience, and particular expertise, as well as developing a reputation that attracts employers' attention. Your personal and professional brand is represented by your branding script. When you use it in the job hunt, networking, and building strong relationships in the community, you will feel more empowered. It's not about having millions of followers or appearing on the red carpet. To become renowned, you must approach your digital life with the intention of establishing the authority, reputation, and audience necessary to accomplish your objectives. This is the first book of its type to show you, step by step, how the world's most successful individuals concentrate their attention, form a plan, and achieve their goals.

The personal brand paradox is a problem that the world is now grappling with. On the one hand, rising global competition is making it more difficult for people to earn enough money to afford the lifestyle that an increasing number of people desire. Social media and the Internet, on the other hand, provide us with the potential to achieve worldwide celebrity. In reality, the millennial generation, who grew up with the Internet as a part of everyday life, now expects to have their fifteen minutes of fame at some point. So, how do you deal with an unstoppable force colliding with an immovable object? "Reinventing And Redefining You" sheds light on branding, which many view as being both an art and a science. However, following these fundamental recommendations might help you get started, especially if you're launching a new business or rebranding. Not only will developing a strong personal brand help you become more well-known in your profession and gain more business.

Only a decade ago, mass-market stores were synonymous with brands. With the rise of social media, traditional companies have become more personal. Social media networks have made it simple to connect your content with consumers. That is the subject of this book. To persuade them to cross the bridge to your content. You'll have the chance to add value and position yourself as an authoritative figure. The opportunity to leave a legacy by making your brand viral, allowing you to transform your business into a cash cow. You'll need a strategy to build a true personal brand. You must learn to utilise social media to its fullest extent. You must be familiar with each platform and the logic that underpins it. I'll reveal the insider secrets and most up-to-date techniques so you'll know which elements to prioritise and which are a waste of time. I promise you that if you follow the ideas in this book, you will have turned your life around in a year and attained financial independence that only a few people have accomplished.

I do mentor, counsel, and train individuals, and I have witnessed firsthand how I have helped others achieve success. This isn't just another book for you to read; it has the potential to completely transform the way you think about success and how you create your business in today's changing times. Building a personal brand is no longer a fad, but rather a requirement in today's competitive economic environment. To distinguish out in the industry, any business owner, entrepreneur, or information provider must use personal branding.

A person's personal brand ought to be an authentic reflection of who you are, what you believe in, and what you want to be recognised for. It must be as genuine as possible. Finally, and most importantly, it must communicate the correct message and maintain consistency across time.

Acknowledgements

At the outset, I will thank my family for supporting me throughout the journey of writing my book and encouraging me to live my dreams; my son has always been instrumental in giving his inspiration to complete the writing of this book. Despite the fact that I am listed as the author of this book,**"Reinventing And Redefining You"** would not have been published if I had depended entirely on my own talents. Creating this book required more than anything—it took a family of dedicated and caring people who were always prepared to lend a hand.

Writing a book while working full-time is no simple task, so I'd want to express my gratitude to my amazing coworkers who act as cheerleaders in equal measure. Thank you, too, to my students and clients for your patience and unflinching support while I worked on this book!

Thank you to everyone who has listened to me argue for doing everything you can to make your life, including your work life, more progressive. I appreciate everyone's assistance throughout the process. This book would not have been possible without each of you having had an impact on my life in some manner.

Lastly, I would like to thank all the people with whom I have been associated. You gave me power. I would like to thank Notion Press for publishing my book. Finally, thank you all for gifting your time to read this book.

I'd want to convey my heartfelt appreciation to the almighty God for bestowing his blessings and being so gracious.

CHAPTER ONE

Reinventing Your Personal Brand

"Your brand is what people say about you when you're not in the room"-Jeff Bezos

What people say about you after you leave the room is your personal brand. Do you want to be in charge of your own brand? Do you desire a deliberate personal brand rather than a coincidental one? A person's personal brand is a determining factor in their professional success. Building a compelling and appealing personal brand is what propels people forward in their professions.

Building rapport at scale is the foundation of personal branding, and rapport-based selling is one of the most basic sales strategies. Experienced salespeople use charisma, also known as personal branding, as a very effective method to complete more transactions with less work.

- Do you want to be in a better position to secure a better job, get more clients, or raise more money for your charity?

- Do you want to be seen as an expert in a way that might lead to a book or speaking career?

Have you ever thought that you are a brand in your own right? Not just in the corporate world, but also in your personal life. You're a genuine brand. But, even if you are, how should you proceed? This book is a step-by-step guide to understanding how you are your own brand and what positive adjustments you need to make in order to grow your brand.

In today's brand-savvy world, you must have a professional viewpoint, and how you might establish one is briefly discussed in this book. Your personal branding statement is similar to your own unique commercial. It informs potential employers and others about you, your abilities and skills, as well as the benefits of how you might contribute to a company, an organisation, an association, or the community. A great personal brand does not happen by accident; it is the result of a conscious effort to define and represent who you are. A personal brand requires active marketing and promotion to acquire exposure and recognition among stakeholders, much like a product does to raise awareness and attract prospective purchasers.

Personal branding is a simple procedure, but it is not easy.

Lead with your ideas! Put yourself in a position of authority! Increase your following! Take control of your own brand! Personal branding is widely mocked, which is not surprising. Strong personal brands thrive at meeting the needs of a specific target. Make sure to identify who your main target audiences are before you begin your plan. The primary objectives you wish to accomplish with your personal branding plan must be in line with the target audiences you have chosen.

Since 2020, many employees have had the ability to change what they anticipate from their employment. In search of greater compensation, more than 40 million Americans left their employment in last two years; the majority changed occupations or shifted positions. While a tight labour market allowed individuals to make more assertive job demands, remote employment assisted some in prioritising their needs outside of the workplace. Many individuals understood leverage to be the capacity to establish emotional separation from their employers and to more clearly define the boundaries between who they are and what they do.

Despite its name, a lot of personal branding advice is written in commercial terms. Jumping into shaping and advertising your reputation, image, and position according to what you believe your audience wants to hear will probably result in a short-term benefit but might have long-term negative effects. This focus on solely marketing your brand might make you seem unauthentic and prevent you from developing genuine connections with others.

Making a polished, superhuman alter ego is not the goal of personal branding. Having a clear idea of how you want to be perceived by others is insufficient. This frequently results in a voice that is unsustainable and unauthentic. Knowing who you are and expressing your story in a deliberate and genuine way are keys to understanding your brand.

There are several concepts you need to comprehend when it comes to personal branding. The first is that you need to understand exactly how it functions, what you can get from it, and how you can develop your brand. For those looking to profit from it, having a recognised name or being prominent in a certain field is highly desired. Numerous chances, advantages, gratuities, and other advantages are brought about by it. It's not only influencers who should use personal branding.

> *Today, anyone can become an influencer, experiencing the best life has to offer while still making money.*

It may be characterised as how you represent yourself and build a brand around yourself rather than a company. By creating a personal brand, you establish yourself as an authority in a certain field. It can assist in increasing social media followers, which helps people land better jobs, sell more goods in their businesses, and attract better employment chances.

People are sharing their expertise, having an effect, attracting chances, and living in "flow"all over the world, in every sector and specialty. They're developing successful businesses and professions while also making a positive difference in the world. These are powerful leaders, and you have the opportunity to be one of them. When it comes to developing a personal brand, people are searching for someone to believe in, someone to be inspired by, someone to learn from, and someone to follow, not just another coach, entrepreneur, or expert.

Your personal brand helps you build meaningful connections and leads to new opportunities because it captures who you are and what abilities you bring to the table.

A person's personal brand has never been more vital. Without one, you will struggle to attract excellent clients, your firm will stagnate, and others will find it difficult to accept your competence. The good news is that you can build your own brand while continuing to do what you enjoy at a reasonable price. Anyone with access to the Internet and social media may amass a large following, establish a professional reputation, and begin attracting clients for their business.

How fast can social media alter people's lives?

There are many examples, but this latest one could be eye-opening. The Kacha Badam song had gone viral on social media. How much are you aware of the humble beginnings of this viral phenomenon? Do you recall that Bhuban Badyakar was the tune's original composer? It would have been difficult for us to trust someone if they had told us a year ago that a song about peanuts would become wildly popular on social media.

However, 2022 has accomplished this incredible feat in just one month, and in spectacular fashion! The song "Kacha Badam" is one of the most well-known social media trends and most popular songs of the year. You probably already know about this catchy song that has captured the attention of millions of Instagram users, unless you've been living under a rock. The sounds of this popular song are currently being danced to by well-known influencers, who are also gaining views minute by minute.

But how was the Kacha Badam song created in the first place? What caused it to become the current sensation? As one might expect, the song "Kacha Badam" came from the most unexpected of places. The song was created by a bengali peanut vendor Bhuban Badyakar. He resides in Birbhaum district's Lakshminarayanpur Panchayat's Kuraljuri village. In exchange for bangles, trinkets, and other valuables, Badyakar travels to adjacent villages and trades peanuts for sale per weight. He uses the Kacha Badam song to draw in new clients and inform them of his presence. A YouTube channel by the name of "Ektara" initially recorded and released the Kacha Badam song. In just two months, Badyakar's modest song has received over 21 million views. Everyone had demonstrated their inventiveness by dancing to the song's beats, from youngsters to actors. The fascinating thing about this song is that the singer is a peanut vendor, not a professional singer. The song's lyrics indicate that he sells untoasted peanuts, and even before the video that rocked the internet, he was well-known in his neighbourhood. Without Bhuban's knowledge, a recording of his song was made and posted online. He expresses gratitude to the person who posted his music, nevertheless.

> *The opportunity to leave a legacy by making your brand viral, allowing you to transform your business into a cash cow.*

He gained recognition quickly as his song became popular all over the world. Celebrities such as Nyla Usha, Rupali Ganguly, Shooter Dadi, and the well-known father-daughter team from Brazil have remixed his reel and created their own versions. Bhuban even worked on a fun remix of Amit Dhull's song, by a Haryanvi actor and singer. The most recent mash-up combines Dhull's Haryanvi lyrics with his own unique lyrics. The popular Kacha Badam music video quickly spread to other websites also, including facebook, and Instagram. Then, singer and musician Nazmu Reachat produced an upbeat remix of Badyakar's songs that got everyone on the internet dancing. As they say, the rest is history. Millions of Instagram users connected with the song about Kacha Badam, or peanuts, making it their go-to commercial. While choreographers contribute their own dance interpretations to the song, food bloggers create dishes for it. Meanwhile, Bhuban Badyakar pleaded with the neighbourhood police to aid him in collecting the compensation to which he is entitled for producing the popular song. The news that Badyakar and Sourav Ganguly featured in a reality programme. It seems absurd, doesn't it? That is the power of the digital age, I suppose.

We are all part of the digital revolution, where individuals become famous in the most unexpected way. Influencers, performers, and trend-setters emerged from Instagram reels and other short video platforms.

There isn't a universal answer for "what works best," because these goals will naturally differ from business to business. Make a list of everything you want from your social media marketing efforts and rank them in order of importance to your company. You can proceed to the next phase once you've determined your primary objectives. This will make it easier to decide which social media platforms will serve your goals the best. For instance, 72% of teens use Instagram, but 18- to 29-year-olds make up the bulk of Twitter users. You may choose to prioritise one social network over another depending on your target audience. Give as much information as you can about your audience's age, gender, geography, hobbies, interests, issues they confront, where they hang out, and other companies they appreciate. The list of details might be endless. By identifying these traits, you can be sure to target them on the finest social networks and create content that will help you achieve your goals. See how everything connects?

As it was previously mentioned, prior to deciding your objectives, you cannot decide which channels to employ or what sort of content to generate. i.e., what do you hope your social media marketing will achieve? You need to be clear about who you're attempting to target in addition to why you're utilising social media marketing. It's crucial to your plan to evaluate the social media marketing activity of your rivals. Considering that they share your target market, spend some time learning about:

- Which platforms they use the most, the type of material they post, and the average level of interaction they receive?
- Which hash tags you will employ?
- What voice modulation you will employ?
- What types of exchanges you will have with your listeners?
- Which call to action do you advocate?

This is a crucial element in any social media marketing campaign, but it's even more crucial if you're working in a group. All information pertaining to a business's social media activity should be covered by brand rules, which should be transparent and available to everyone with access to the social accounts.

Making sure everyone is on the same page and outlining these aspects early on in your social media marketing plan can help you develop a consistent and recognisable brand identity on social media. All social media marketing activity has to start with a strategy before launching into a few tweets and Instagram posts. By taking the time to conduct this social media marketing study, you'll be in a strong position to choose the platforms that are appropriate for your audience and your goals and gain insight into the online behaviours of your target market. After all the previous planning, you should now have a very clear sense of which social networks are most beneficial to your business. While all social media platforms might offer some advantages to all businesses, striving to be overly active on all of them will cause you to stretch yourself too thin. Instead, prioritise which networks are best for your audience and your company's goals and concentrate on creating a variety of content types to maximise outcomes. Instagram should be your first pick if you sell a consumer good that is well-suited to visual marketing. On the other hand, if you offer B2B services, Twitter or LinkedIn will likely be more successful for you.

Effective personal branding will set you apart from the competition.

What if I told you that changing your life's trajectory didn't need a lot of willpower? What if I told you that a few minor shifts in your thinking could mean the difference between staying trapped and living the life of your dreams?

Don't be concerned. This book will not merely tell you to create objectives or to dream big! Those words may seem great, but they make no difference. You see, you won't be able to change your circumstances unless you become someone capable of doing so. Some experts will advise you to demonstrate grit! or summon the courage to triumph.

What do you cherish, and what do you hold true? What particular perspective do you have on the world? Your personal branding journey should begin here, and the short-term discomfort will result in long-term value. Finding your essence requires a lot of effort. You will establish a far more meaningful and long-lasting connection with your audience if you are aware of your values and motivations. You'll be aware of the message to convey and have a framework for decision-making. You may remain loyal to yourself and be authentic by having a strong sense of your own identity.

Branding, traditionally, refers to the essence or identity of a company, an item, or a service. When done right, branding serves as the foundation for your whole company since it derives from your beliefs and goals. It serves as the foundation for a company's whole reputation. A brand communicates, "This is who I am and why I'm here." Connection is evoked by brand; it is what you remember about a company, a service, or a product, whether or not you made any purchases. It is ultimately what creates devoted consumers. Marketing, which is about promotion and activity, is the how, while branding is the why. Finding, attracting, and interacting with customers in order to influence their behaviour is the goal of marketing. Although marketing is short-term and response-oriented, branding is long-term and response-oriented.

"Your brand is your public identity, what you're trusted for. And for your brand to endure, it has to be tested, redefined, managed, and expanded as markets evolve. Brands either learn or disappear."– Lisa Gansky

When the epidemic struck India in early 2020, I suddenly found myself with a lot of free time to invent and build new things in my life. I had a clear aim of writing management books to leave a legacy, and I knew that this year would force me to accomplish things I had never done before or ever dreamed of doing. Yes, I produced four management books before the epidemic struck India, but I never had enough time to think of contemporary topics that urgently needed to be addressed. I want to guide my readers through a process of acquiring greater clarity about how they want to build their own presence without feeling overwhelmed or trapped, so this book takes an excitingly informal and action-oriented approach to personal branding.

I take a casual yet excitingly coachable approach to the idea, which grabs the reader's attention and encourages them to take action. You all know that achieving success is a journey, and you are now on that path. It was created by you . As a result, you have the ability to create a noticeable presence. This book has the potential to tackle a pressing issue that many entrepreneurs encounter on a daily basis: how can you attract clients in order to run your business? In the end, it's all about putting your money where your mouth is and focusing on certain areas of your brand to establish a strong one. When you're not around, your reputation is what others say about you. It's your most valuable asset for advancing your business, advancing your profession, and having more flexibility in many areas of life. Too many individuals, though, leave it to chance. It's a closely guarded secret: being the greatest isn't enough; you also have to be recognised as the best. Your brand is your brand, your one-of-a-kind selling factor, and the reason people choose you over the competition. Words like "brand awareness" is frequently used and signal success and a solid presence in your industry, especially when thousands of competing businesses are fighting for your consumers' attention. You obviously understand the importance of building your own brand, but few people can tell you how to get started. That is the subject of the book. It's written in such a way that by the time you get to the end, you'll know precisely what to do to create a brand. Individual marking has been shown to be a successful strategy, and it may also help you get an advantage in your job search.

Fortunately, you can look into how many successful people have used individual marking to figure out what it is and how it might help you. In the present day, branding is not as complex as it once was before the advent of social media. Today, social media has aided you in innumerable ways that you could never have anticipated. Because of the easiness with which social media has made your lives, many of you have become celebrities throughout the world. Even if it seems simple to you, avoid any possible gaffes by identifying the topics your company should never discuss on social media in the rules. These are just a few instances; the list might be much longer depending on your business and the number of social networks you use for marketing. Remember that the most essential thing is to follow your rules, no matter how you choose to represent your company on social media. Make sure your activity is consistent across all social networks since you want your audience to feel a sense of familiarity that will inspire loyalty.

We live in a multicultural society where people of all ethnicities, religions, and backgrounds coexist. These individuals are connected on a shared platform via social media, which brings them together. Therefore, encouraging a sense of togetherness encourages the growth of communal ties. As an illustration, foodies may join the community of food bloggers, gamers can join gaming-specific groups, etc. The greatest way to express sentiments and ideas is through social media, whether it be through a song, a poem, a piece of art, a sumptuous dessert, or anything else. Anyone may use the platform to share their ideas, which will be seen by millions of people. Sharing creative efforts with others may pave the way for success and a number of landmarks. Although it might be challenging to know where to begin, try to consider your target audience and truly get to the core of what matters to them and what they are most likely to react to. This selection should not be too tough if you have done comprehensive market research on competitors and demographics.

The burden of social media marketing is enormous, especially if you use a variety of platforms.

Without proper planning, it is easy to post infrequently or ignore specific social networks. By using a social media marketing calendar, you can see how frequently you are posting and maintain consistency in your posting, which is the best way to stay on top of all this information. You may prepare in advance for significant occasions or milestones, business announcements, or pertinent social media holidays by using a content calendar!

You must schedule content if you want to save hours of work and generally improve the quality of your social media marketing. You may bulk upload your images, videos, and text posts for Instagram, Facebook, and Twitter using an automated management and scheduling platform and schedule them to go live in the coming weeks! By keeping everything organised and freeing up more time for content development and other creative components of social media marketing, scheduling social media material in advance increases efficiency. Finally, but certainly not least!

Monitoring the metrics and KPIs related to your goals for each social network is one of the most crucial elements of social media marketing. It's great to produce top-notch content and interact with your audience, but you won't discover what works best if you don't pay attention to the data. A Facebook campaign may seem fantastic to you, but if it fails to achieve its goals, it is a waste of time and money. By monitoring key indicators, you can build and optimise your activity and thrive in social media marketing!

How will you design your personal brand story?

Adults' attention spans today range from seven to twelve seconds; therefore, it's imperative that we capture and hold their attention right away. So, how do we go about doing that? Consider your most recent conference experience or the most interesting podcast or webinar you've ever listened to. You probably recall the anecdotes and first-hand accounts more than the statistics and numerical data that were presented.

The power of storytelling is contagious, and it turns out that our brains are built to recall stories rather than facts. Therefore, incorporating it into our brand assets and content marketing initiatives is in our best interests. We can develop trust while also more effectively relating to and connecting with our target audience through storytelling. And this is what you want your story to do. Your prospective client needs to have a clear picture of who you are, what you've conquered, what your present objective is, and what makes you credible after reading it.

Now, every effective personal brand narrative has a few essential components that work together to make the tale come to life. I refer to these components as the "three Cs." The first C stands for character, which makes it simple to include in your personal brand story as the character is, of course, you. You should identify yourself and give the background information that establishes the narrative for where you were before the conflict arose at the beginning of your story. What were you doing just before the one significant event that ignited the development of your present business? Conflict is the second C. It needs some suspense to build up in order to pique attention and curiosity. Here's where you'll need to become personal because people don't relate to butterflies and rainbows. You must show vulnerability and divulge the trying situation that finally led to your breakthrough. Your target audience should be able to fully connect with this conflict. They should conclude by adding, "I understand how it feels." Or, "That's my current difficulty." The final crucial element is the conclusion. The most effective resolutions express the conflict's outcome clearly and show the "aha" moment, "breakthrough," "change of viewpoint," or "discovery" that inspired your present goal and company endeavour. Here, you may discuss the lessons you've taken away from your battle, the solutions you've found, and how you've been empowered to assist others overcome their obstacles and reach similar success. Keep in mind that the goal of your personal brand narrative isn't to make a lot of sales. The objective is to connect your experience to the audience's problems and show how you can be the answer. You become more recognisable and trustworthy when your audience can identify with you as a genuine person and learn from you. And the desire to know you better and collaborate with you will grow among your audience

Are you where you want to be personally and professionally?

Reinventing oneself is essentially a process of self-transformation. The process of transitioning from who you were to who you are and finally to who you want to be. This may appear to be a simple procedure, but it may be really complex in practice. Resistance sometimes arises as a result of your need to cling to the past. Because as things change, you must make way for new things, which necessitates the release of old items that are no longer required. Relationships, friendships, careers, clothing, locations you live in, and so on are examples of these things.

"Branding demands commitment; commitment to continual re-invention; striking chords with people to stir their emotions; and commitment to imagination. It is easy to be cynical about such things, much harder to be successful." – Richard Branson

It is a common thought. Or who are you if you don't have a blank? Can you guess what the most common worry you hear from people who are reinventing themselves is?

You are so afraid of failure, especially when you are plunging into the unknown, not knowing if you will fall or soar. A lot of your anxiety stems from how you'll be seen by your friends, family, and coworkers if things don't go as planned. You could see their worry for you in their eyes. Is it possible that you imagined everything that could possibly go wrong? This may even feel like a grieving process for some, but it is vital, and I encourage you to start right now. Begin to explore your emotions and be honest with yourself. After all, it's for your own benefit. Also, keep in mind that the world changes quickly, and you may be compelled to let go if you wait too long. With experience, you'll be able to let go more quickly and create more possibilities for reinvention.

Have you ever had a family member or a well-intentioned friend warn you that a job you were considering wasn't a safe bet, or a well-intentioned friend urge you to stay in your safe 9 to 5 because the danger of trying anything different was too great? You frequently underestimate the significance of external influences on your lives and professions. Your friends, family, and society all want you to feel safe and secure, yet their views may all too easily become your own truth. You begin making decisions based on those ideas without recognising that they are choices that are not your own.

Failure is difficult, and you all want to avoid it; it's human nature. However, in order to establish a personal brand that stands out from the crowd, you must first fail. When Walt Disney reflected on his failed early attempts at developing an animation brand, he frequently mentioned this. When you're young, I believe it's critical to experience a good hard failure. That taught me a great deal. Because it makes you aware of the potential consequences. And the worst-case scenario is never as terrifying as not trying at all. You'll never get the greatest brand unless you fail a few times while pushing yourself out of your comfort zone. The finest brands are always the result of repeated trial and error. Written material or video are two of the greatest ways to share that tale online. Simply use your smartphone to video message clients, establish a personal relationship with potential clients, and communicate with coworkers. After all, you're never without your smartphone!

"A brand for a company is like a reputation for a person. You earn reputation by trying to do hard things well." - Jeff Bezos

To establish a personal brand that successfully expresses your personal and professional identity, you must first understand yourself. After some contemplation, make a list of your own strengths and shortcomings. If you're having problems answering these questions, ask your friends, family, and coworkers for their opinions. Remember that many people are afraid to choose a specialty because they don't want to be restricted. Recognise that your personal brand, like many business brands, will develop as your career grows. Whether you're attending a networking event or a casual party, having an elevator pitch prepared makes it straightforward to explain what you do and where you're going (or would want to go) in your career. You need to come up with incredibly brief, succinct things to say—stories to tell that frame your strengths in the right light. While your story should be similar across all platforms, understanding where your target audience is most likely to go will help you focus on telling your best story there. The more connections you make and the more value you can provide in your interactions, the more probable it is that your personal brand will become well-known.

Your personal brand will be more engaging if you can add more color to your story. Everyone (nearly) needs a personal brand. So, rather than it happening by accident, intentionally developing a personal brand for yourself allows you to have a voice in how you promote yourself and offers you control over crafting an authentic picture of your personality. While social networking sites are mostly used to interact with others in a social setting, they may also be used to start creating your own brand. Your personal brand should be built in such a way that it can be simply stated in an online context, as well as orally and via actions and behaviors. Because you'll be living and breathing your personal brand, it's critical that it's real and truthful. Make contacts, make decisions, and plan career moves that are consistent with your brand.

"Thought leadership happens when you're willing to have your brand stand for more than what you sell "– Seth Price

When it comes to the press and media, too many people are unfocused, attempting to be everything to everyone. What I advise, decide what your essential message is and adhere to it. It will be much easier to both develop material around your personal brand and have others define you if you keep your message focused on your target audience. Be sincere. It will make managing your own brand on a daily basis much easier. Your personal brand should be a simple everyday filter through which you generate content and communicate with your target audience.

Be a master of your specialty, talent, or business before launching a personal brand.

Then your material will aid in furthering your identity. You establish a reputation as an expert in your area while simultaneously enhancing that notoriety on social media when establishing your own brand. If you're an expert in one field, your reputation will be enough to help you establish the brand you desire. Consistency is comparable to having a limited focus—much it's simpler to become known for a single issue if you develop content and brand language around it on a regular basis. Make sure your personal brand promise is consistent online and off. You must be consistent in your speech, gravitas, and physical presence. Don't overlook how little errors might undermine the efficacy of your own brand. So, whether you're establishing a crazy, out-there entertaining brand or one that's a little more on the conservative side, consistency is key.

However, you must narrow down the universe of prospective viewers from everyone to these precise people: those who are seeking someone who is just like you, with your talents, qualities, and beliefs. Once you've determined who your target audience is, things get even more complicated since people have two sets of demands. You have both functional and emotional requirements. To show you what it looks like, I'll use a retail scenario. Let's pretend I'm looking for a cup of coffee or a delicious snack. I can go to a Starbucks and, sure enough, there is coffee there. Isn't it true that they have wonderful treats? Your functional requirements have been satisfied.

Consider the last time you visited an excellent restaurant. Did that restaurant provide a wide range of cuisines? There's no way you can be a personal brand for everything. Your differentiator will help you build a niche for yourself. So take some time to consider your area of expertise. What is your area of expertise? What are some topics on which you are uniquely equipped to speak? You may begin to direct your brand to deliver considerable value to others after you realise your expertise. Create your own distinct differentiator- Finding your distinct differentiator does not have to be difficult.

> *"An authentic and honest brand narrative is fundamental today; otherwise, you will simply be edited out." – Marco Bizzarrif*

I'll teach you how to get yours in simple steps. To begin, consider the characteristics that identify you and where you are in life. Age, race, hair color, and other characteristics are among them. You have your work and lifestyle on top of those more obvious characteristics. This includes the industry you operate in, the job you do, where you reside, and what degree of education you have. Choose which characteristics are both novel and distinctive to you. Your own experiences and perspectives on life are ultimately what set you apart from others. Second, consider your abilities. Any language you speak, a unique pastime, or a cause you care about are all examples of your abilities. It also doesn't have to be limited to a single language, interest, or topic. Finally, consider your destination. Perhaps your collection of talents isn't entirely distinct from those of the competition.

Find out what motivates you. To create a personal brand that accurately portrays who you are, you must first define your motivations. For individuals, developing a personal brand might lead to new job chances. Others may be more concerned with being a thought leader in general. In any case, knowing your motives can aid you in developing a powerful brand narrative and a long-term brand strategy. I'd want you to do the following. Consider where you'd like to see yourself in a year or two. Assume you have a successful personal brand that is readily identifiable. What are your plans for utilising your own brand? Perhaps you'll use it to speak at additional events, land new clients, or launch your own business. In any case, keep in mind that the goals of your personal brand should represent who you are today and who you aspire to be in the future.

Your personal brand strategy is driven by your motivations.

Let's work together to create a true personal brand for you. It's time to assess your motives and determine what you hope to gain from developing a great personal brand. The Golden Rules — If you Google "how to develop a personal brand," you'll find infinite blog posts, listicles, and a slew of misinformed YouTube videos. Here's the reality: Because even though the process is unique to you, there are no exact lists or set-in-stone criteria for developing a strong personal brand. Remember that just because a process works for someone else doesn't mean you have to follow the identical procedures.

Now I'd like to share with you my golden guidelines for personal branding. First and foremost, you must be sincere. It's not about putting on a show when it comes to building a personal brand. An inauthentic individual may be detected from a mile away. The most successful personal brands are never built purely on celebrity or visibility, and despite what you may see on social media with the emergence of social media influencers, you must work hard to succeed. Set yourself up for success by being authentically you. Next, prioritise your connections since they may lead to opportunities, and opportunities are precious. One of the most untapped sources for expanding your personal brand is the sheer number of opportunities accessible to you because you invest in your own network. Take the time to carefully cultivate and sustain such connections. Now think about being consistent. Consistency is essential for having a unified voice. This will assist you in becoming a thinker. If you work in finance and want to establish your brand in that field, for example, focus solely on financial content. If you stick to that one issue, you'll start to develop thought leadership. Also, express yourself in your dealings with people. The elevator pitch for who you are and what you do should be perfected.

Here's a suggestion: In most conversations, your aim is to persuade customers to believe in your brand's story. Set a clear brand direction and let others know where you're headed, and they'll be more willing to help and support you. Finally, don't be scared to change your mind. Just because you've committed to developing a targeted personal brand doesn't mean you won't continue to evolve, learn, and reshape your identity. You frequently worry that your brand will be like a corporate logo, difficult to modify once it's out there, but a brand is much more than a logo. Because personal brands are linked to individuals who are continuously changing, they change. Recognise that your brand will change over time, and be strategic about picking a lane and sticking to it until you need to pivot. Creating a brand narrative: Every successful brand has a backstory.

You must have a distinct story and history that defines who you are and what you want to accomplish, just like any excellent business. A story is the foundation of your own brand. In order to establish a great brand story, it's critical to take stock of where you've been from and where you're going. A good origin narrative includes some struggle. You relate to problems more easily than anyone do to victory. Have an open and honest dialogue with yourself about your brand narrative. These are the two questions you should ask. What event or season in your life separates your life into Before and After? Perhaps it was before you obtained your first dream job or after you graduated from graduate school. Second, what obstacles did you have to face to get to where you are now?

Now it's time for you to start writing your narrative. Write a first draft of your brand narrative on a piece of paper or in a notebook, or on your laptop or iPad, using these guidelines. To begin with, the best stories are those that include other people. Return to your story and include genuine people who had a significant impact on your life and work. Through those other people, your viers will be able to relate to your narrative. Make them relevant by emphasising characteristics that will be important to your target audience. Second, the best stories are interesting to read. You are all susceptible to boredom, and in today's fast-paced environment, you have a short attention span. Examine your story and break it down into four bullet points. Third, stories elicit strong emotions. Examine each bullet point and make the necessary changes so that each one elicits an emotional response from your audience. Fourth, tales must come to an end. The audience wants to know what happened at the end of the narrative. What did they get out of it, and why did they receive it? Finish your story by connecting it to your personal branding objective.

Writing your own brand narrative is a lot easier than you would believe. Don't worry if it's not flawless. Put pen to paper or start typing to develop a version. You'll return and continue to update your narrative as your personal brand evolves. Describe your brand's history— When was the last time you were told a truly amazing story? You've all got a buddy who has a terrific tale about a vacation they took, an unexpected event that occurred, or a very gorgeous puppy they peted at a party. Your DNA is made up of stories. They're how you share values, communicate, and learn from one another. The finest ones capture and retain your attention, and no tale is more compelling than one about you and your own path. You have your own unique brand narrative to tell. Narrative is one of the most effective strategies to develop a captivating personal brand. It's simple to express who you are and what you do professionally, but a dull description of yourself will not help you stand out from the crowd. Consider what makes your narrative unique:

- Did you travel a circuitous route to get to where you are now?
- Has your career taken any unexpected turns?
- How have your life experiences influenced your career decisions?

Building a real narrative is the most successful personal branding technique these days-single character monologues are boring and much more boring for your personal brand. No one wants to hear you yell about your business into the abyss of social media, so construct a story around it that your audience can become involved in. After you've established your own brand and created a following, the next step is to consider the legacy you'll leave behind.

A personal brand is a never-ending undertaking that develops and evolves.

A lot of effort goes into building a strong brand narrative, but having a great tale to tell isn't enough; you also need to become an expert at delivering it. Telling your narrative over and over is the best approach to becoming a skilled story teller. You should put in some practice time. And if you practice, you'll not only get better at delivering your narrative, but you'll also reap additional rewards. For starters, it assists you in truly embodying the identity you're constructing. Hearing yourself narrate your own narrative will help you mentally draw the connections between where you've been and where you want to go. Next, understanding and telling your narrative from beginning to end boosts your confidence. You don't have to be concerned about being put on the spot. You will be able to shine if you have a prepared narrative to tell. Here are some suggestions for telling your brand's narrative. Keep the tale simple and straightforward.

- Find those modest brag occasions to let your organisation's influencers know what you're up to and how you're succeeding.
- Recognise that you have a personal brand at work; if you embrace it, you will have more influence over your career. So, according to popular demand, here are my top LinkedIn suggestions for owning your own brand.
- To begin, leave a remark at least five times every day. The more you remark, the more likely you are to appear. And the more you put yourself out there, the more your talent and brand become well-known. Next, make sure you have a catchy headline. The first thing people notice when they see you is your headline.

According to John C. Maxwell, "one of the greatest values of mentors" is the capacity to look ahead of others and assist them negotiate a path to their objective. It's tempting to want to develop a strong, personal brand on your own when you're just starting out. After all, it takes a lot of personal work to construct your brand narrative, find your objectives, and deal with issues like impostor syndrome, but as Maxwell points out, you need assistance navigating. A mentor is a critical form of assistance that you will require in order to be successful in your life. Over the years, I've had various mentors from whom I've acquired many useful things.

Having a mentor has a number of advantages. For starters, they can assist you in avoiding mistakes. A superb mentor has been there and can assist you to avoid making a mistake or signing a terrible agreement. Mentors also help you become more creative and productive. They assist you in gaining access to an outside perspective that provides you with inspiration for new ideas. Mentors also connect you to a larger network. Mentors are frequently personally involved in your success and eager to link you with those who they believe can help you achieve even greater success. Finally, they assist you in hearing difficult realities.

You need someone with a fresh viewpoint in your life who can give you honest comments and help you develop. Mentors are an excellent source of candid, constructive criticism. Everyone, especially C-level executives, needs mentors, no matter how successful they are. Therefore, make finding a mentor or several mentors a major priority. Mentors to choose from: It's crucial to realise that finding a mentor isn't a one-size-fits-all situation. You naturally want to get along well with your mentors, but chemistry isn't everything. Finally, you require individuals in your lives who will not simply give what you want to hear.

Your mentor is there to not only support you, but also to give you the harsh facts that will help you improve yourself and move closer to your objective. You should avoid your own personal prejudices while choosing a mentor. Using criteria-based decision-making is a fantastic approach to do this. This is how you do it. First, you must determine what attributes a mentor must possess in order to assist you in achieving your personal brand objectives.

- What information do they require?
- What are their priorities?
- What kind of communication style do they have?
- What is the status of their availability?
- Who is in their network?

Take your time to consider everything. Write down all of the attributes that are essential to you, then prioritise and rank the must-haves. Mentors that are accomplished, driven, honest, and available are what you want. The next step is to find someone who you know will be willing to mentor you.

Create a list of people who meet your must-haves by looking through your network and everyone in your extended network. Inviting a mentor to mentor you is the final step in the mentoring process. It does not have to be difficult. Simply make a short and basic request.

Let them know what your major, overarching aim is and how excited you would be to have them as a mentor. Tell them why you'd like to work with them as a mentor. This covers the personality attributes you appreciate as well as the aspects of their overall biography, background, or job experience that you are most interested in. Then, express your readiness to listen to their candid and open comments. You're not seeking someone to correspond with. You're looking for someone who can provide you with constructive feedback and strategic advice.

So, what do you have to lose? Get out there and find a mentor for yourself. It's also critical that you submit material on LinkedIn on a regular basis, and this information can be of any sort. A brief update, a lengthier forum, a written piece or article, a video, or even a sharing of anything related to your area, along with a brief statement of why you believe it is significant. Then, when you publish, make a point of mentioning and tagging people. Shutouts are popular on LinkedIn, and referencing others broadens your network and increases exposure to your postings.

"Too many companies want their brands to reflect some idealized, perfected image of themselves. As a consequence, their brands acquire no texture, no character and no public trust."– Richard Branson

You want to provide value to your audience every time you post on social media. Don't worry about how many posts you have or attempting to boost your weekly post count. Prioritise quality over quantity. If you have a lot to schedule or will be out of town, another alternative is to utilize a social media planner. To keep it short, focus on a few crucial things to mention in your elevator pitch. If you want to reach out to hiring managers and recruiters, for example, you may start by creating or upgrading your LinkedIn page. This might mean you're seeking a new job, have expertise in a certain field, or have just enhanced the worth of your present department or firm. It's critical to network consistently (and successfully) to expand your professional circle while you develop your ideal personal brand.

Attend formal and casual networking events to meet colleagues and industry thought leaders. Remaining accessible to hiring managers, coworkers, and others—even if you're not looking for work—is one of the most crucial components of personal branding. Because there are so many different social media platforms accessible today, your online presence will most certainly vary based on the channel you pick. Additionally, if you want one of your sites or accounts to be only for friends and family, change your privacy settings to ensure that potential employers don't come across any material that might jeopardise your job search.

Because networking accounts for 85% of all job openings, attending these events on a regular basis can help you not only grow your brand, but also improve your career. Don't be afraid to invite fellow guests to meet up for an educational interview or a casual coffee chat after the event. Remember, if you don't have a chance to meet up at the event, send an email or connect on LinkedIn to start a dialogue. One of the simplest and most successful methods to create your personal brand is to have current and previous coworkers and bosses support you. This allows people to articulate your worth to you. You should nurture your own evaluations in the form of recommendations, much as a corporation may create customer reviews and testimonials for use in sales and marketing content.

LinkedIn is an excellent site to seek endorsements since these suggestions are likely to attract the attention of potential employers. However, don't forget to ask those supporting you to serve as an actual reference throughout your job hunt, making sure they're prepared to talk with a potential employer or write a genuine letter of recommendation if necessary. Don't know who to ask? Former supervisors who closely supervised you are great, but other connections, such as academics and leaders of organisations you belong to, may also create good recommendations. As you become older, you should reinvent your own brand. Your personal brand will grow as the digital ecosystem changes and your career progresses.

Adjust your persona as you meet new people, discover new networking opportunities, and advance in your career. Don't be afraid to establish a brand that allows you to shine as long as it reflects your professional life. Remember to emphasize what sets you distinct from others while establishing your personal brand, such as your unique hobbies, values, professional experience, and educational background. If you have a master's degree, for example, you may use it to set yourself apart from other experts in your industry and display your knowledge.

To define what it means to be successful, to challenge your inner perfectionist and accept your true worth. High achievers, for example, frequently define success as faultless execution, oblivious to the fact that there are various levels of success. Consider a project you're working on. Make a list of how it would appear if you executed it flawlessly and then failed badly. Then determine what constitutes an exceptional, good enough, and ordinary performance. It's a loud world filled with a lot of information, and things are always changing. It's easy to get lost in the shuffle. In any sector, I have a proven strategy for standing out and becoming an industry expert. I've given talks on personal branding and communications and interviewed amazing thinkers. It's a way of repaying the favor. It's also one of the most effective strategies to distinguish yourself and expand your personal brand. Consider the following scenario: you have a friend who operates a restaurant. And you have a buddy who employs a large number of people and frequently provides catered lunches.

A networker would strive to connect the two of them, but only if they received some sort of reward or financial advantage. If you're a connector, though, you see two strangers who can benefit each other in some way, such as one receiving delicious meals and the other gaining some business. And you don't have anything to do with that opportunity. Sun Tzu, the author of "The Art of War," once stated, "Every fight is won before it is ever fought." This statement is one of my favorites, and it reminded me of the importance of vision for success. When you imagine what you want to achieve ahead of time, you can then take action to make it happen. Rather than scurrying about like a hamster on a hamster wheel, you're now working smart. The first step is to close your eyes and ask yourself, "What is that one-year objective that you want to achieve now?"

If the internet is an essential component of modern life, social media is an essential component of communication that cannot be avoided, especially for those who lead busy lives and rely on it for even the tiniest updates. On a variety of platforms, people may keep in touch with friends, family, and the outside world. Social media use is one of the most popular online hobbies, and 82% of Americans had a profile on one or more social networking sites in 2021, up 2% from the 80% usage rate the year before. By 2022, there will be around 273 million social media users in the US.

If individuals could go back in time just a little bit, the

genuine beginnings of social media may be found in blogging, where the first accounts appeared somewhere in the 1980s. After that, more social opportunities were produced by the development of free platforms and chat rooms. Later, it was transformed by Facebook, Twitter, and other sites.

Nowadays, we can't even begin to envision a world without the various social media platforms since social media has already ingrained itself into our daily lives. Since everyone is aware of how important social media is for small, medium, and large businesses, I will concentrate on the person and how social media impacts our life in this chapter. Social media has both good and bad aspects, just like anything else, therefore it has both positive and negative affects on us.

How to build a brand called "you"?

The most important thing is your unique brand. In this book I will explain what distinction is and how to figure out what makes you exceptional and unique to your target audience. In this chapter, I will tell you how to find problems you can solve for others through empathy and active listening, as well as how to construct a concluding statement in your value articulation that will make you genuinely memorable.

"Your brand is a gateway to your true work. You know you are here to do something – to create something or help others in some way. The question is, how can you set up your life and work so that you can do it? The answer lies in your brand. When you create a compelling brand you attract people who want the promise of your brand – which you deliver." –Dave Buck

Personal branding is the process of consciously shaping and influencing an individual's public impression. There are several investigations into growing awareness and its deeper meaning. Time is compressed to create a fascinating trip that leaves you yearning for more of your true nature. Every single one of your favorite influencers began with zero followers and had to make several errors to get to where they are now—earning more money each year than their parents did a decade ago.

However, in order to become a top creator, you must first comprehend the Insta-ready lifestyle's techniques. This is accomplished by establishing them as an industry authority or by setting them apart from the competitors. Personal branding is the most effective technique to demonstrate your distinct qualities, specialisations, and selling factors. It includes all of the methods you use to market yourself and your company's public image. Personal brands are no longer limited to A-list celebrities and talk show hosts. Anyone may now achieve internet notoriety by developing their personal brand.

Make sure they are saying something positive! I will explain why it's essential, and how to build a powerful online brand for your company. How Does It Work? Personal branding is the process of consciously shaping and influencing an individual's public impression. This is accomplished by establishing them as an industry authority or by setting them apart from the competitors.

Personal branding isn't a capitalist marketing ploy devised to profit from starving artists and despondent individuals lost in the maze of self-promotion. In marketing, advertising, and communication, branding is defined as a combination of qualities and characteristics that identify and differentiate a brand from the rest of the world.

Branding is as much about content as it is about context, and it never lives in a vacuum.

Personal branding encompasses a variety of factors, including your beliefs, style, look, presence, and influence – in other words, your personality. Contrary to common belief, personal branding does not begin with your online appearance or website design. It certainly appears in more visible manifestations at some point. It undoubtedly appears in more outward appearances at some point, such as visual design and style, but the source of it is you. It all starts with you: your personality, values, beliefs, and unique style. While defining your own brand, you do not need to go through a branding process. Because discovering what you truly stand for, how you can add value as a person and how you can be useful is more important than developing your brand.

The term "personal brand"is well-known in the world of social media accounts. The majority of people, on the other hand, are unaware that successful public personalities have been branding themselves for decades. So, what exactly is a true personal brand? Answers to the following questions can be found inside:

- Why is it more successful to take a comprehensive approach to personal branding?
- What sets successful public people and businesses apart?
- What makes you truly happy?

There's a common misconception that personal brands are simply for self-promotion, but you'll learn in this book that a self-brand may help you live a more meaningful life. This book is for everyone who wants to improve their life, get to know themselves better, and take control of their narrative. Every entrepreneur will tell you that success requires hard work and perseverance. One of the most essential things you can do is establish your own brand and reputation, in addition to loving what you do, learning from others, and assembling a fantastic team around you.

I will guide you on how to clarify your goal and specialty, that "one thing" for which you want to be recognised. You can dentify and comprehend your target audience, the people you wish to inspire, instruct, and attract. a clear, powerful message that engages and connects with your target audience with considerable success via brand building.

Create a solid content and social media strategy to help you bring your brand to life; learn how to increase your productivity and efficiency so you can 'find the time' to build your brand; your strategy for building the online reputation you want people to see; the hidden ideas behind affinity audiences, attraction marketing, and cause marketing; a step-by-step explanation of how to build authority online using the best tools, platforms, and resources, with real-world examples.

However, remarks like this don't delve any further. I know you have what it takes to make a positive difference in your life. Because you're looking for strategies to improve right now. You'll get the answers and insights you've been looking for if you take a chance on yourself and read the book. You continuously fantasise about a better future, yet you feel helpless to make your fantasies a reality.

You look back on your life and think, "How did I get here?" or "Is this it?" You can't let go of the past and ruminate on what you could have done better. You've tried and failed to change more times than you can remember. You want to make your life better, but you're not sure where to begin. The psychological roadblocks that prevent you from changing (and how to fix them) Why does goal-setting fail? How to discover your passion (even if you don't think you have one)? I will provide you with essential insights and exercises to help you put what you've learned into practice. You'll become an active participant in your own development rather than merely reading about it.

Your self-presentation is divided into two stages, according to Erving Goffman's self-presentation theory: The "front stage" is the manner in which a person performs in public or among other people in order to project a specific image of themselves to others. Celebrities and sportsmen prefer to establish their own brands on the front stage, displaying a plethora of positive, purposeful messages that attempt to depict them in the way they would like to be viewed. In contrast to what Goffman refers to as the "backstage," which is a person's behavior when they are not in public or not posting on social media, aiming to create a persona or brand that they want people to recognise.

Personal branding is the most effective way to position yourself as a subject matter expert. It enables you to take advantage of high-volume exposure while maintaining a clear position on corporate objectives, values, and ambitions. Having a professional and well-known brand can help you gain new clients. Customers are more inclined to buy from you if they are familiar with you. Personal branding, on the other hand, fosters brand loyalty, dedication, and community. This may result in improved client connections and more repeat business.

According to research there are different sorts of personal brands like noble category of those individuals are well-known for assisting others and donating their time to charitable causes. This includes Angelina Jolie, Dolly Parton, and Bill Gates. Go-getter another type of personna and they prioritise success over everything else. This type of personal brand is recognised for providing knowledge and becoming industry thought leaders. This category includes Elon Musk, Jeff Bezos, and Simon Sinek. Hipsters are those brands frequently blend compassion and careerism, but they are more concerned with knowledge exchange than action. Look to this brand for innovative and fashionable items. Contentious are those brands distribute stuff in order to stir up debate. They may not agree with the stuff they share, but they like stirring up controversy. This might include your favorite news reporters or meme accounts. Adapters are those individuals enjoy bringing people together and taking pride in the creation of communities. They are typically innovative and love other people's approval. Consider your favorite Instagram celebs or influencers. Selective brands only share information with select groups of people. They are resourceful and take the effort to curate material for their audience. You know what your unique brand is and how to use it.

"Personal branding is the art of becoming knowable, likable and trustable."– John Jantsch

Look at the Instagram's impact on how we live now. It began as a photo-sharing website but swiftly became the most significant app of our time. The hardships and oddities of the folks behind Instagram are being made public in a forensic new book. Instagram impacted the world, not simply how technology was seen. As the most popular social media firm to date, Instagram has been a monstrous force in many of our lives. In many respects, it established the standard for social media platforms and had a significant influence on how we interact with technology and one another. It's understandable that a platform would have such a lasting influence on society and the IT sector.

Instagram was one of the first platforms to demonstrate to the tech industry what genuine platform interaction looked like. Instagram has continuously been the strongest platform for interaction in the history of social media, whereas Twitter and Facebook had hit-or-miss periods with their audiences (where engagement functioned in peaks and troughs based on the current occurrences of the time).

This involves getting more individuals to like and comment on images as well as follow one another more often. What is most surprising? It doesn't seem like this will slow down any time soon. Instagram regularly adds fresh reasons to participate, which is a significant reason why engagement has remained so strong on the platform over time. There are several other tools they've introduced that help users connect with one another, from the advent of AR filters (more on this later) to contributing reactions to articles. And the level of participation on the platform doesn't appear to be slowing down any time soon as long as they keep pushing the limits.

The emergence of photography is one of Instagram's most notable contributions to both technology and world culture. While this has helped the cameras on smartphones get better, Instagram has also spurred the market to develop more advanced camera parts. Simply put, everyone became a photographer as a result of the software, which was obvious even in the early stages of its usage. Instagram removed this obstacle, making photography much more accessible. While there will always be specialists in the field, this made it much simpler for the average individual to enjoy taking pictures. Leaving an enduring impression on the business, this is one of Instagram's most proud accomplishments.

While it may seem simple to purchase Instagram followers and declare yourself an influencer, there are many hassles involved in branding using this strategy, which unintentionally fueled the growth of personal branding on social media. Influencer culture is here to stay as the new cultural spokespersons, giving individuals a platform to interact with folks they identify as being similar to themselves. The rise of the influencer is the largest transformation Instagram has brought about in the IT industry. Influencers are essentially voices in primarily narrow groups that advocate for various products, services, or locations, which has become quite popular in every market from weddings to fashion. Filters gave individuals more confidence in what they could accomplish on Instagram and served as a basic building block for picture modification. This improved average, in turn, inspired individuals to create more material.

People found it difficult to interact with augmented reality before Instagram began to realise its full potential. While Snapchat was the first to debut features like Face Filters, Instagram truly embraced the idea of augmented reality and made its potential available to everyone through their Story platform.

Social media, in my opinion, has two sides. It has numerous good impacts but also many harmful ones. Due to the scarcity of reliable information sources, one of the main issues with modern online public opinion is the gap between it and reality.

In today's digital world, millions of individuals, including students and young job seekers, fight for the same positions, clients, and consumers. For instance, according to Kinsta's data, LinkedIn has 810 million users, 57 million of whom work for recruiting organisations.

Personal branding is a terrific approach to selling yourself and your profession to a certain audience or industry. Additionally, it could have a really favourable effect on your work life. Building a personal brand, for example, might provide you a competitive edge over other job hopefuls who don't have a strong internet presence. Give use whatever your objectives, personal branding may assist you in achieving them. Let us look at the positive side of social media first.

- It may make friendships stronger. According to research, 29% of social network users think that using social networks makes them more outgoing and cheerful (only 5% of users expressed the opposite feeling), and 52% of teenagers who use social media say that it strengthens their friendships. Only 4% of teenagers claim that their friendship has been damaged by social media.
- People are more likely to recognise you and believe in what you do if you have a unique personal brand. Additionally, if you brand yourself as an experienced professional, they will naturally trust you more.

- When you are regarded as an authority in your field, it is much easier to win over the trust and confidence of potential customers. There is a lot of competition as a result, but recruiters will be interested in candidates that have a strong personal brand. Making a lasting impression and standing out from the crowd may be easier with personal branding.
- It could give them a feeling of community. According to research by Griffith University in Australia and the University of Queensland, although American students nowadays have fewer friends than their counterparts in the past, they feel less lonely than they did before. They are more sociable and don't feel alone, in part due to their use of technology.
- It enables kids to behave well. Children may connect with several significant events and individuals from across the world via Twitter, Facebook, and other sizable social networks. Children are aware of the influence of their voice, and they may do a variety of activities, such as anonymously post encouraging remarks online or collect funds for individuals in need.
- According to a recent Pew Research survey, social media is the primary source of political news for roughly one in five Americans. The survey also reveals that individuals who largely rely on social media for their political news are often less knowledgeable and more likely to come across unverified claims than those who acquire their news from conventional sources.
- It can support kids' self-expression. Both producers and actors may satisfy the requirements of self-expression through social media. Children may cooperate with faraway collaborators and share their work with broader viewers thanks to digital technology (basic skills in the

21st century). Social media can also give feedback to help you know whether they're sincere.

- New career possibilities, speaking engagements, sales leads, etc. will become available thanks to a strong personal brand. This makes perfect sense given that, according to CareerBuilder research, 70% of employers evaluate candidates using social networking sites like LinkedIn. Additionally, if you have a strong personal brand, employers are more likely to locate you and get in touch with you about employment openings. But a personal brand may also draw collaborators, fans, and voters (if you are a politician). Depending on the industry you work in, there are different options.

- Social media now has a far greater impact on political campaigns than previous forms of media. Election politics are becoming more and more dependent on social media, as shown with Howard Dean's ultimately failed 2003 run, the election of the first African-American president in 2008, and Donald Trump's Twitter-driven campaign. According to The New York Times, "The victory of Donald J. Trump is arguably the starkest demonstration yet that social networks are helping to radically rewire society worldwide."

- The advantages of having kids interact, share, and learn online are now clear from new studies. As a parent, you can encourage these good traits, acknowledge the significance of social media for kids, and assist them in discovering methods to truly enrich their lives.

- Personal branding may assist you in bringing in new clients and consumers, whether you're an artist, independent contractor, business owner, or small business owner. According to Harvard's longitudinal study, approximately 60% of customers are more inclined to make a purchase from a brand they are familiar with. If you have a strong personal brand, prospects are more likely to identify your name and what you do. Due to their excellent experience, customers are more inclined to use your product or service frequently in the future.

- Social media has a significant impact on employment and recruitment. Anyone trying to make a name for themselves in their field should use professional social networks like LinkedIn. They enable the development and promotion of personal brands. 19% of recruiting managers base their hiring decisions on information obtained from social media. 70% of companies use social networking sites to study potential employees, according to CareerBuilder's 2018 social media recruiting survey.

- Candidates for jobs are far more employable if they learn the newest and most cutting-edge social media tactics. A 2020 survey by OnePoll on behalf of Pearson and Connections Academy asked 2,000 U.S. parents and their high school-aged children about the "new normal" of high school. 68%t of students and 65% of their parents believe that social media will be a useful tool and part of the new high school normal. Blogs, wikis, LinkedIn, Twitter, Facebook, and podcasts are now common tools for learning in many educational institutions. Social media has contributed to the increase in long-distance online learning. Despite issues of lack of privacy and some instances of cheating among long-distance learners, this has not deterred social platforms from being used in education.

- Focus on developing a personal brand that reflects the values and qualifications the organisation is seeking in candidates if landing a job there is your ultimate aim. If you are a politician, you want more people to support you and vote for you. If you want to draw in more customers, concentrate on creating a personal brand that speaks to them and what they want from a company.

- A personal brand strategy will be adapted to each person's wants and goals, regardless of the goal. It's time to study the procedures involved in getting started after discovering the benefits of personal branding.

- Since social media is a relatively new technology, determining its long-term positive and negative effects can be challenging. However, a number of studies have found a direct link between frequent usage of social networking sites and a higher risk of depression, self-harm, anxiety, and loneliness.

- Social media encourages people to develop and value "social media connections" over real friendships, which is one of its repercussions. On social media, the word "friend" is a flimsy substitute for actual friendship. Real friends have a personal connection, regularly engage in person, and truly know each other.

- One of the most important advantages of social media is connectivity. Numerous users can be connected at any time, anywhere. Social media's connectivity and ability to disseminate information internationally might facilitate human interaction. It generates international connections.

- It is admirable that social media is being used in schooling. To promote constructive learning, learners and instructors can sign up for international collaborative platforms. Social media has experienced meteoric growth during the last 10 years. In 2005, there was very little activity in the sector. The majority of them were not aware at the time, and among those that were, having a MySpace profile usually meant complex backdrops and distinctive playlists rather than a direct link.

- Use social media to keep up with happenings around the world or in other people's lives. Social media, as opposed to television, radio, or newspapers, enables everyone to correctly communicate information by portraying a genuine image. It helps to present real-world news internationally.

- Social media may be used to publicise noble actions. It is the perfect instrument for supporting causes, such as sending money to cancer patients who need it for treatment.

- Social media is a tool that anybody can use to help people financially, but it is also the quickest and easiest method to advance any great cause.

- Social media has helped people become more aware of their actions. By acting as a conduit for information, it opens up opportunities for creativity and success by expanding their knowledge and skills. Global events are extensively covered on social media, increasing people's awareness of their surroundings. By encouraging knowledge and creativity, it also helps with skill development.

- Social networking is a fantastic way to decompress. People who are struggling with stress, sadness, and loneliness can find assistance in a variety of groups. These communities can foster a happier mindset and support the formation of positive interpersonal interactions, both of which will improve mental health.

- Social media enhances business connections by encouraging user goodwill; its promotion boosts sales, which in turn boosts profitability. Customers' reviews and comments are an invaluable resource for businesses. Companies may benefit from increased popularity and revenue as a result of user-accumulated likes.
- By offering products and services and asking for feedback, social media improves client involvement. Users from diverse groups provide a variety of comments and recommendations, which might help to please them and improve areas of focus.

Without social media, social, ethical, environmental, and political injustices wouldn't be as well known. The balance of power has shifted away from a select few as a result of concerns becoming more widely known. Facebook is currently used by almost a quarter of the world's population. Nearly 80% of internet users in the US use this platform. Social networks gain influence as they expand because they depend on human connections. Do you find any flipside of social media? Let us look at those aspects also.

- Because of the internet, anyone with opposing views can now discover that others share them. And when these people connect with one another on social media, they may do things like make publications, memes, and entire online universes that support their viewpoint before it is widely accepted.
- From a child's point of view, it feels like there is news concerning child pornography, cyberbullying, or feeling left out every day. Social media does have hazards.

However, youngsters use and think about social media in a variety of ways that grownups are unable to comprehend. Only a small minority of the millions of youngsters who use them are misusing them. Therefore, I continue to believe that social media's benefits exceed its drawbacks.

- On the other hand, "slacktivism" is progressively killing off actual activism as a result of social media. While social media activism raises awareness of societal concerns, it is yet unclear if this awareness is leading to substantive change.

- Some contend that social sharing has enabled people to voice their worries about social issues online and through mobile devices rather than needing to actively participate in campaigns in person. They just contribute by clicking the "like" button or sharing material.

- When individuals are presented with alternatives that relieve them of the need to take action, they often respond in a passive manner that is very human. According to 2013 research by the Sauder School of Business at the University of British Columbia, when given the chance to "like" a social cause, individuals often choose to donate their time and money to it instead. On the other hand, people are more inclined to provide significant assistance by making a financial gift when they are permitted to do so in secret.

- Peer pressure may be a contributing factor in the recent tendency for political polls in the U.S. to misread voter intentions: respondents may give answers that they believe the pollsters expect or that they believe will please their peers, but in the privacy of the voting booth (or at home with a mail-in ballot), they cast their ballots in accordance with their true preferences.

- Due to the popularity of social media, it is uncommon to come across a company that does not use at least one social media platform to connect with its clients and potential clients. Businesses understand how important social media is for connecting with consumers and increasing sales.
- The study indicated that whereas private donations are made because the cause is in line with one's principles, public donations are made to appease the opinions of others. Businesses have come to understand that social media can be used to gather insights, increase demand, and develop specialised product offers. These tasks are crucial in both the realm of traditional brick-and-mortar enterprises and, obviously, in e-commerce.
- According to several studies, establishing social networks at work can improve information exchange. As a result, project management processes are enhanced, and specialised information may be shared. Boundaries and silos are removed in the workplace when social technologies are fully implemented. This increases contact and contributes to the development of more highly competent and informed personnel. On the other hand, a small number of social "shares" might result in poor social proof and undermine the legitimacy of a firm.
- It's interesting to note that despite the fact that social sharing is now more commonplace than not in business, some organisations have gone against the flow and removed the social sharing buttons from their websites after personally experiencing some negative social media repercussions.

An e-commerce store from Finland named Taloon.com conducted a case study and discovered that by removing the share buttons from their product pages,conversions increased by 11.9%. These findings demonstrate how social media's influence has a two-pronged effect. Products that garner a lot of shares can boost sales. However, when the opposite is true, people start to doubt the brand and the business. This impact is known as "social proof," according to psychologist Dr. Paul Marsden, author of "The Social Commerce Handbook."

Now, change happens more quickly. For instance, the development of mobile technology has had a significant impact on social media. Mobile devices are the most popular around the globe in terms of total minutes spent online. They enable everyone to connect at any time, from any location, and using any device.

> *The development of social media over the past 20 years has marked a tremendous advancement in information and communication technology.*

Social media sites that you use often might make you dependent on seeing what others are up to. FOMO (Fear of missing out) is the exacerbated belief that others are having a better time or living better lives than you. You find yourself constantly checking your notifications in an effort to alleviate this discomfort. Teenagers feel the drive to excel, be popular, and fit in. Even before social media, this procedure was difficult. When you include social media platforms like Facebook, Twitter, Snapchat, and Instagram, teens are now under pressure to mature too quickly in the online world.

In a 2019 study conducted by the Cyberbullying Institute of middle and high school students in the United States, it was discovered that more than 36% of respondents admitted to experiencing cyberbullying at least once, with 30% reporting experiencing it twice or more. Additionally, it was shown that almost 15% and nearly 11%, respectively, acknowledged cyberbullying someone twice or more. Social media tools may be abused by teenagers to propagate rumours and upload films. It can offer genuine assistance. Whether a marginalised youngster is interested in a strange subject that isn't at all "popular" or is having problems identifying their gender, the Internet's tolerance can be of assistance. Even high-quality internet support is available for teenagers who have suicidal tendencies. Users from the entire online community once used voice conferencing software on a forum to convince a youngster to abandon suicide ideas.

- Some of the risks encountered by social media users include stalking, identity theft, personal assaults, and information abuse. Most of the time, it is the users who are at fault since they reveal information that shouldn't be made public. The misunderstanding of how an online profile's private and public sections truly function is what causes the confusion. Unfortunately, it's frequently already too late when private stuff is destroyed. challenges in both people's personal and professional lives as a result of the material.

- Emotional ties are hampered by social media. Everything is communicated digitally through letters, which might stifle expression. When people who would normally visit one another to say hello only send texts instead of hugs, creativity is lost. Quick wit is rare due to the decline of in-person discussions and true face-to-face talks. Due to the negative impacts of social media on people's mental health, their sense of humour and athletic tête-à-têtes have been affected, and they no longer experience feelings of love, friendship, pleasure, or happiness.

Networking sites help brands become more well-known. Users are more likely to pay attention to visually appealing content and items, which enhances brand awareness and increases consumer understanding of specific products and services. Being "present" and in the moment while spending time with one another is important. Make memories by talking to one another about the past, present, and future when friends and family get together. Unfortunately, today, with social media being available on the cell phone, individuals spend time with each other "reading" through posts.

Words and voice are used to transmit sentiments, but in order to do so successfully, one must be physically present in front of the other person. When someone uses them in a text, social media alters the colour of it, hiding the true meaning. Because families cannot spend quality time together, social media has strained many relationships. Family time has suffered as "me" and privacy have taken primacy (due to the quality of texts that appear on social media). False information and rumours spread easily, leading to depression and suicide. People that interact on social media are apathetic and do not blink an eye when they need to injure someone. The most recent trolls, critical remarks, and feedback are all examples of the callousness that has developed as a result of social media's invisibility.

The weakness of social media has also shown how easy it is to collect someone's data. To prevent such circumstances, privacy settings must be regularly updated and profiles must be closed. Impulsivity permeates social media. The continual need to check your phone for new messages, notifications, and updates can be distracting. Even disregarding critical tasks, the person wastes time by focusing exclusively on the unimportant update. Obesity, stress, and high blood pressure are a few health issues that emerge from spending hours on the sofa hooked to our smartphones. Due to a lack of physical exercise or access to social media, technology and related platforms have caused an increase in laziness among people. Cyberbullying has affected people, especially youngsters, by readily trapping them in threats, scams, and other harmful behaviors. Addiction to social media among young people is a severe problem that has had terrible results.

While sometimes checking social media and using a smartphone is okay, excessive use saps productivity. People are now embracing social media as a dating and marriage platform. The likelihood is that the information on the site is fraudulent, which might ultimately result in a toxic relationship or even a divorce. Public perception is not always reliable and accurate. Differentiations between the two exist. Another type of public opinion that occurs in society and has an impact on it is unfavourable and incorrect public opinion, such as false information and rumours.

The Internet has grown to play an increasingly significant role in ideology as a result of the breadth, speed, openness, sharing, and interaction of online media. People with ulterior purposes frequently utilise online public opinion to propagate false information, hype sensitive news, and hype social hotspots, which causes misunderstandings within online groups, leads to the creation of rumours, deceives netizens, and misleads the public. Information, as has been said, is a powerful thing. People cannot use the power of information if it cannot be shared. Social media has a favourable effect on how knowledge is shared in the modern world. Information may now be accessed thanks to platforms like Facebook, LinkedIn, Twitter, and others.

What method of personal branding is the most successful?

The first step in anything is to understand who you are and what you want to be known for. Choose your USP (unique selling proposition). Determine your area of strength and use it to establish your USP. It should be a topic that interests you specifically and that your target audience finds interesting. While how you say something is equally as important as what you say, Coca-Cola, for instance, was one of the first companies to include personal branding in its marketing plans. The brand demonstrated the lifestyle that consumers wished to represent and created a distinctive identity based on the ideals of joy, experience, community, and happiness.

Prior to creating a personal brand, you must define exactly what you want from it. What do you want to achieve? What goals do you have? When you are clear on your goals, you may focus on creating a personal brand that will support your achievement of those goals. It's time to do some research now that you know what you want. This step is crucial because it will enable you to comprehend the state of the market and what you must do to differentiate yourself.

If you are a musician, for instance, your primary target audience will be those who listen to your music and those who enjoy your musical taste. On the other hand, if you are an expert in climate change, your target market may include those looking to learn more about it, future employers, or other professionals in your sector who you would like to collaborate with. Spend some time defining and considering the demands of your primary target audiences. This will enable you to speak in a way that appeals to them.

As with any marketing approach, knowing who your rivals are can help you position yourself more effectively in the marketplace. The following are the two most important steps you must take:

1) List all the individuals or groups that compete with you or share your goals in order to identify your competition.

2) Determine what they do and how they do it. Are there significant companies in your market? What services do they provide? What are their advantages and disadvantages?

There are numerous things that you might pick up from your rivals. You'll have a better grasp of what you need to do to stand out if you analyse both your competitors and yourself. Your brand has an online and offline presence. It is advised to go through the results of a Google search for your name. If nothing happens, it's not always a bad thing. You have the power to influence what people discover when they conduct an online reputation search. Another smart move is to inquire about your relatives' opinions of you and what makes you special in their eyes. Evaluate yourself from your own point of view.

- What are your advantages and disadvantages?
- What skills do you possess?
- What facets of your character or areas of expertise would you like to emphasize?
- How do you want people to see you?
- What are your company's purpose, vision, mission, and values?
- What is your brand positioning statement, often known as your value proposition?
- What sets you apart from the competition in your industry?
- What products or services do you offer that no one else does?

Name, personal narrative, personality, visual identity, and communication style make up a brand's identity. Keep in mind to deliver on your promises to your audience and to be consistent with your personal brand across all of your media. You'll win your readers' respect and trust by doing this.

A personal branding statement might be useful when using this kind of technique. It serves as a technique to condense your unique qualities and goals. It need to be concise, easy to comprehend, and straight to the point. You may consider it your major pitch. Making a personal branding statement is not difficult. "I'm a professional illustrator who loves poetry and photography." Making a list of your areas of expertise and goals should come first. Distil it down to one or two phrases that best capture who you are and what you want to accomplish.

Personal branding statements are frequently found in the bio area of social media sites, but they are also useful when introducing yourself to various audiences offline.

You are now prepared to create a plan for your personal branding as a consequence of your previous efforts. You may use this as a guide to develop and maintain your brand.

These illustrations show that personal branding statements don't have to be difficult or excessive. They need to be a clear description of who you are and what you hope to achieve. By using a tagline, you may improve your own branding statement. A tagline is a brief, memorable sentence that encapsulates what you do and what makes you unique. When used properly, this kind of branding approach may help you gain more awareness, credibility, and possibilities. I'll now reveal all the ins and outs of personal branding and discuss its significance for both your personal and professional lives.

To begin, decide on a topic where you are an expert! It's extremely crucial to determine your niche and then attempt to appeal to your target audience or a segment of the market where you may rule supreme with the appropriate methods. One must first select a niche and work toward it by concentrating on three things in particular—vision, consistency, and professionalism—in order to develop a successful personal brand. The secret is to stand out by sharing your narrative, showcasing your personality, and making connections with those who share your goals.

By establishing oneself as the authority or subject-matter expert in a specific industrial specialty, one may increase their credibility and level of trust with their target audience. This makes your brand more approachable and linked to the target market. People who are familiar with you and your company will have greater faith in you and purchase more goods and services from you. Additionally, they are more inclined to recommend you to others.

Try searching for yourself on Google for a few seconds if you're still unsure of your own brand. Whenever your name appears in print, it represents your brand! Online users already have a personal brand that is well established. Your personal brand is influenced by your social media profiles, websites, digital portfolios, blog posts, and other forms of communication. Make yourself visible to others by optimising your profiles and communication channels with SEO keywords and phrases related to your industry specialisation, role, or intended outcomes. This will make it easier for people to find you online.

Use these guidelines to build a strong brand for yourself in order to reach more people and win them over. Your personal brand needs a strategy to be successful, just like any other brand. These are the most effective methods for differentiating your brand from the competition.

You must be extremely clear about the services and values you will offer before developing a brand for yourself. Find out what makes your abilities, talents, and strengths unique. Any brand that wants to succeed must first understand its audience. You need to understand how your abilities can draw in a potential audience. You can develop and carry out plans more efficiently if you are aware of your brand's target market.

By regularly producing material that appeals to your audience, you can keep your social media profiles current and relevant. To be credible and memorable, you must also maintain consistency with your ideas and the methods by which you convey them. To increase your reputation within the target audience, use social media every day to scan, filter, read, connect, write, and answer. Such initiatives entail changing the emphasis from viewing social media use as a possible hazard to viewing it as a professional benefit in the digital era.

It's important to know exactly what you want your brand to stand for. People these days tend to go through things too quickly and give their brand the shortest amount of time possible. The first stage of effective personal branding is setting objectives and having a clear message about your brand for your audience and yourself. This tendency can cause someone to become a "jack of all trades, master of none."

With a consistent voice, tone, and appearance across media, let your brand speak for you. It may be done by creating a clearly defined and unified presence, message, and appearance that is simple to recognise and remember. Fonts, logos, colours, photos, and the brand positioning statement are all visual identity and branding elements that should be consistent throughout all online and offline accounts. Be consistent with your approach and your strategy.

Your brand may soar to greater heights if you are open and honest with your potential customers. Without a lot of the facts provided, the majority of consumers do not depend on a dubious brand. To win the audience's trust, be extremely explicit about your brand, what it offers, how it offers it, and how it differs from the competitors. Make connections with those who are appropriate for your brand. It may be rival businesses, prospective clients, or well-known figures in related industries. To raise the profile and trustworthiness of your brand, get in touch with them about working together.

Regarding the services you are offering in your sector, be extremely detailed. Knowing what your rivals don't have to offer can help you better choose what you can. It might aid in laying the groundwork for your brand. In this day and age, finding clients without a demonstrated portfolio may be rather challenging. Utilise social media channels to advertise and reach people with your services. By posting articles on your expertise, a blog is another excellent technique to gain the audience's trust (if your brand permits it).

If there is one thing you can do to promote and develop your online brand, it is this. A blog makes it simple to express your ideas, display your portfolio, and communicate with other online influencers. Make sure to develop and post the greatest material that you possibly can, including text and video, so you can establish a dedicated audience around your blog, which will be useful for you to grow into a major brand in the long run.

A highly effective strategy for attracting clients is to tell a story through your brand. The narrative may touch on the history of your brand, how you set yourself apart from competitors, or the benefits of using your brand. Humans are drawn to stories that relate to us or provide solutions to our issues. Strike a balance and develop your unique brand narrative. If it's a paid application, social media for freebies might attract an early audience. Service providers may make themselves easier to locate through their websites, blogs, and YouTube videos connected to their brands. You may increase your reach by running ads on Facebook, Instagram, LinkedIn, and other well-known social media platforms.

A wonderful approach to engaging with your audience and uncovering areas for development for your business is through feedback. No matter how well-known a person's brand becomes, audience input is important. Because of this, practically all major brands put the consumer experience first. Great personal branding may mean different things to different people and different businesses. The way a person talks, acts, and portrays themselves is known as their personal brand.

To build a successful personal brand, it is essential to comprehend the strategies of your direct and indirect competitors and the factors that contributed to their success. After establishing your objectives, determine the gap between what your competitors are delivering and what you can do to fill it. Find a different strategy to deal with this problem if the rival brand excels where yours cannot. Using social media efficiently is essential to achieving success, regardless of whether your personal brand incorporates a website, an application, or any other medium. Sell the audience on the things you can do better than your rivals and the reasons they should give you a chance.

With the proper strategy and execution, personal branding may help you gain clients in the current era of advertising. But if you begin the process of building a brand for yourself without the right support, it can become rather daunting and confusing. Whatever the motivation, list three to five objectives you want to accomplish with your personal brand. In the event that you (inevitably) don't feel like blogging one day, this will motivate you to keep going and help define your content plan.

People like communicating with other people. When your target clients feel more intimately linked to you, it is simpler to earn their trust. Even while you may want your personal brand to be all about business, it's useful to occasionally display your human side. Mention your relationships with clients, coworkers, or employers. Share material from leaders you admire and individuals in your network. You give folks a glimpse of who you are by providing stuff that isn't always polished — a person who is looking to connect with others. Make sure they're saying something positive because, as Jeff Bezos so eloquently put it, "Your brand is what people say about you when you're not in the room." By utilising the power of technological breakthroughs to build your personal brand, you may position yourself for success in your job and beyond.

Your contemporary CV is your own brand. Employers are seeking applicants with that extra something that makes them distinctive in a world where everyone has a degree. Who knows you is more important than who knows you. People and companies are more likely to offer you collaboration possibilities and professional progress if you become an authority in a certain specialty. Once your brand is well-known, it will be easy to draw in customers who will spend more.

For anyone advancing their career, taking into account personal branding may be quite beneficial.

The key to successful personal branding is making sure that your target audience knows who you are, what you stand for, and what makes you different from your rivals in a certain market sector. The secret to success in the digital age is personal branding. Being a member of the digital era, when people's attention spans are decreasing by the minute, makes it difficult yet more crucial than ever to create an impact. "Personal branding" is the enduring impression that separates one from others. In order to expand their services and information, people use personal branding to share their special blend of knowledge and experiences with a community of people. In order to interact with potential clients, increase visibility within the business, shape one's reputation, and create a lasting impression through online and in-person networking, one has to have a strong personal brand.

In today's digital age, it's simple to self-publish a book on Apple, Amazon, and your own site and earn money from it. This is an underutilised strategy for developing your own brand. Almost everyone on this list, whether you realise it or not, has authored at least one book. Everyone has at least one best-selling book on Amazon or the New York Times, from Pat Flynn to Neil Patel to Grant Cardone. In addition to the financial gain, writing and publishing a book may enhance your personal brand and advance it if it is a success.

One thing Nathan Barry of ConvertKit often advises is to "teach all you know" in order to develop a successful business. Don't hold back, and be sure to impart as much of your expertise as you can. You'll see that practically everyone on the list of folks we've included in this piece teaches something. Grant explains sales techniques, Neil Patel on content marketing, and so on. Not only is sharing what you know with your audience a terrific gift, but it will also help draw attention and, in the long run, revenue.

Everyone can teach someone else something. Decide what you can teach people that will aid in your long-term personal brand growth, and then constantly practise it. When everyone else is moving in one direction, it is always preferable to choose a different route. Whether your goal is to develop your own brand or launch a successful company, you must forge your own path. Think big, be original, and be sure to absorb lessons from your errors. You can only achieve greatness and motivate others in this way. After all, there is no use in developing and growing your brand if you can't motivate others to take action.

When failure is seen, most people become paralyzed. Even in terms of personal branding, the same is true. Don't give up on developing and increasing your personal brand if you don't get outstanding results.

One does not become a personal brand overnight. Before you see the results, a lot of preparation and effort are required. Everyone, though, is competing for the same attention. There are a lot of you vying for the same focus. Just like a professional brand, you have to plan strategically and appeal to your target demographic.

Anyone who wishes to achieve their goals and advance their profession must focus on building their own brand. If you develop a powerful personal brand, you'll leave a lasting impression and win people's respect and trust. So give your personal brand some thought and watch the chances come your way. It's likely to be time well spent. Enjoy every moment you have left on earth. encounter everything. Take care of your friends and yourself. Enjoy yourself; be wild; be odd. Go make a mistake today! You might as well like the procedure since you must. Discover the root of your issue and solve it to learn from your mistakes. Be a great example of being human; do not attempt to be flawless.

No matter how hard you concentrate on reputation control, ultimately everyone comes out as they really are. Every behaviour and action reveals who you are, your genuine values, and your convictions, and this is the lived experience of your brand. Make an effort to figure out who you are so that your perception of yourself and others is congruent. Work to ensure that your words and actions are consistent. Personal branding is just that.

Add your brand to your daily activities. Before anyone else, you should be the first and most devoted user of your brand. Never forget that your name is your brand. The audiences you are attempting to reach will judge you on how you act, how you speak, and how confident you are in the products you offer.

The Ultimate Guide To Redefine You

"If people like you they will listen to you, but if they trust you, they'll do business with you."– Zig Ziglar

Your personal brand helps you build meaningful connections and leads to new opportunities because it captures who you are and what abilities you bring to the table. When you're deliberate about building your brand, you'll be amazed at who contacts you. But there's a lot more to it. In this chapter, I will expand on the necessity of developing a personal brand and offers practical advice on how to do so, even if you've never considered it before. While most people think of brands as being associated with businesses, everyone has one. Consider what others say and think about you. It includes both your abilities and who you are, and it's how you set yourself apart from the competition. What you stand for and what you do are both part of your brand. Consider well-known brands such as Apple or Nike. They do, in fact, sell goods. They're more than that, though. They reflect particular feelings and ideals. The finest personal brands are distinct, genuine, and dependable.

*"Personal branding is about managing your name —
even if you don't own a business — in a world of
misinformation, disinformation, and semi-permanent
Google records." - Tim Ferriss*

Do you want to learn more about personal branding? Do you realise the significance of a brand, let alone personal branding? If you haven't already, this is the book for you. It's a short, easy-to-read book that offers helpful advice on personal branding. It not only explains what it is but also provides countless examples of how to accomplish it. It's chock-full of examples of how to approach the concept and how to properly market oneself. It's an excellent resource for job searchers, small business owners, and individuals who want to publicise their products or themselves.

It talks about the social media mania that's sweeping the globe, as well as your offline interactions. This is a wonderful book for everyone who has an internet presence, especially if they have one. Your personal brand does not have to be a company, and it may be utilised to advance your career. The methods you're employing to develop and manage your personal brand have a purpose other than revenue. They also allow you to develop an influential presence that you can use in your profession on a daily basis. You gain on both sides when you invest in your own brand. You win by increasing your company's value, and you win because a stronger brand makes you more valuable outside of it. As you advance in your profession and incorporate what you've learned into your consistent and focused brand image, you increase your chances of success.

*"If you don't give the market the story to talk about,
they'll define your brand's story for you." - David Brier*

Anyone may now achieve internet notoriety by developing their personal brand. Make sure they are saying something positive! What Is the Importance of Personal Branding? Consider a few of the most well-known household names. Winfrey, Oprah. Musk, Elon, and Ellen. Each of these individuals has a distinct and widely recognized personal brand. Oprah is known for her kindness, Musk for his technological prowess, and Ellen for her wit. You can even get the impression that you know them personally. At the absolute least, you are interested in their work because of their status as public figures.

You were all confused by the 2020 epidemic, and you began to question the fundamental meaning of your life—what normal do you want to return to? Do you like to live completely in the moment, on your own terms, no matter what, or do you prefer to live in terror of what could happen? Start evolving and unlocking your true potential equips you with the knowledge you need to go deep and reclaim your lost authenticity, power, and ownership of who you truly are. Stop looking for answers outside of yourself, and let go of your need to be repaired or rescued. It's all in your head.

"Great companies that build an enduring brand have an emotional relationship with customers that has no barrier. And that emotional relationship is on the most important characteristic, which is trust." – Howard Schultz

Personal branding is the most effective technique to reach a wider audience and develop a worldwide image. Customers want to feel linked to you, and this connection aids in the development of trust. Do you recall when personal brands were reserved for celebrities and huge corporations? Actors, entertainers, Fortune 100 companies, and sportsmen received all of the attention and ruled the airwaves. Almost anyone willing to put in the time and effort these days may become a "thought leader" in a certain sector. Of course, it won't happen overnight. Just a fast Google search will reveal how regular individuals from all over the world are utilising new personal branding technologies, notably social media, to create personal brands that draw tens of thousands of visitors to their websites and social profiles.

"Your personal brand is a promise to your clients... a promise of quality, consistency, competency, and reliability." - Jason Hartman

Personal branding has gained popularity in recent years as the job market has gotten increasingly competitive. But what does it mean to have a personal brand? Essentially, it's a means for others to learn more about you, including your professional ethos, goals, and mission. You've all heard of celebrities having a personal brand. Consider Oprah Winfrey, Steve Jobs, Beyonce, Lizzo, Richard Branson and a slew of other celebrities and politicians. They've all developed a public character—a personal brand—that allows others to gauge their personality. Beyond the hoopla, though, branding oneself is a crucial concern in the workplace. Because of the internet's pervasiveness and the rise of social networking sites, it's become critical for every professional with an online presence to mold and manage their personal brand. Because it is a representation of you that people see when they search for you online as well as the image you choose to project in face-to-face encounters, your personal brand is crucial. Whether you realize it or not, your online behaviors—whether on LinkedIn, Facebook, Twitter, or other social media platforms—establish a searchable online personal profile.

Who are you? and Who do you want to be?

Everyone, including you, has a personal brand. It's what people think of when they hear your name; what comes up in a Google search for you; and your social media presence. It's vital to deliberately create your personal brand and establish one that will help you succeed in your profession and life. A strong personal brand may lead to new chances and connections that can alter your life if done correctly. Building a personal brand, on the other hand, isn't easy. While you may wing it and hope for the best, the finest brand builders are planned, niched-down, and most importantly, consistent. This book is for individuals who, regardless of how much self-work or awakening they have done, are ready to claim their liberation from life's illusions, who are dying to live with no idea how.

"A brand is the set of expectations, memories, stories and relationships that, taken together, account for a consumer's decision to choose one product or service over another." - Seth Godin

Developing a personal brand is critical if you are looking for a promotion or changing professions or fields. You may obtain a clearer picture of what you want to achieve and how you need to be viewed to achieve it by building a brand for yourself and then advertising those traits to your target audience. Developing a personal brand might seem like an impossible endeavor. And not knowing where to begin is one of the most common ways to get lost in the process. Even Oprah Winfrey experimented with many styles on a tiny local program before establishing her voice as one of the world's most prominent personal brands. When looking for a job or establishing your own business, it's both useful and vital to stand out in your look-at-me culture and changing employment market.

There are basically two ways to continue to expand your personal brand once you've created it over time: either jump over others and burn bridges, or slowly grow a community around your brand. Maintaining a cheerful attitude and assisting people will only help your brand develop in the long term. If you pay attention across many social media platforms rather than focusing primarily on one, you may be able to creatively deconstruct social statistics and identify the next big trend. Separating your personal brand from your personal life, as previously discussed, is one technique to make developing a personal brand tough for yourself. While it is possible, it is simpler to develop a personal brand when you are first starting out. Your personal brand should accompany you around at all times. It must be a true reflection of who you are and an amplification of your beliefs. With this in mind, your personal brand reflects not just a variety of work tasks such as marketing, finance, or creative, but also values such as giving back, intelligent leadership, and mentorship.

Why is empathy important for your personal brand?

There is no visible distinction between the two stages in the strongest personal brands. There are no two personalities, one for public affairs and the other for private affairs. Not wearing masks or adopting numerous identities contributes to a strong personality and personal brand's authenticity and believability. There is no slipping into or out of the role, and the two stages can not be mixed. Every facet is influenced by a single personality. Empathy is Oprah's most prevalent personality trait. It shows brightly in every public appearance she makes. It distinguishes her from the rest of the pack. Her words, tone of speech, and body language all reveal this. It comes from the way she tells stories and assists others in telling theirs.

Personal branding is all about adding value and expressing a narrative. Empathy is the capacity to sense other people's emotions and to understand what they are thinking and experiencing. Empaths are compassionate, kind, nurturing, big-hearted, and generous people. They are extremely perceptive and possess a high level of emotional intelligence. They are the ideal friends—the ones who will always be there for you, listen to you, and care about you. You cannot comprehend the viewpoints of others.

Empathy is the ability to connect with others by understanding their needs, goals, and feelings without them directly expressing them.

You must be able to connect with every type of audience in order to give value and become relevant. You need to understand what value and utility mean to them without their having to tell you. Listening, observing, detecting patterns of behavior, and responding to feedback are all part of the process. to value and promote diversity. Empathy enables you to treat individuals on an emotional level while also assisting you in letting go of prejudices, labels, and biases. A person who is really empathetic can relate to a wide range of individuals because they value variety in all its forms, regardless of gender, age, or socioeconomic standing. It doesn't contradict the idea of providing value to a narrow audience; rather, it emphasises how you may foster variability within a specialty while being approachable. You feel and relate to stories because they help you feel less alone and heard. It gives you personal encouragement and determination to keep going when someone understands and understands what you're going through. You are here to belong, and any indication that you do is a good sign.

Are you doomed or attractive in the digital world?

You had no influence when you were born. You were born on this planet without any preconceived notions. Your parents are your first and arguably most powerful influence. Innocent phrases meant to protect you, such as "don't play much with water," if repeated often enough, can stifle your willingness to take chances, while more explicit ones, such as "art work isn't a vocation," might deter you from following your aspirations. After that, you'll look at the educational system. One that forces you to choose only one item to commit to. You may be urged to choose societally dependable courses like science or math in order to increase your chances of success.

Alternatively, you may be influenced by the professional choices of your peers. The online world is a great area for your own brand to take shape. Through social media and social networking, you are now connected to a worldwide economy. It's not a fad or a trend that will fade away. Social media is a powerful tool for communicating your ideals and offerings to people all around the world. Let's go over some of the fundamentals of social media as they pertain to personal branding. First and foremost, it is critical to be authentic online. This isn't the place to pretend to be someone you aren't or to dress up as someone you aren't in the hopes of seeming better or wiser. You want to put your own brand principles on display and show people who you are.

In 1997, a website named "Six Degrees" was founded as the first social networking platform. It allowed users to build a profile and then become friends with other people. The internet transitioned from Six Degrees to the era of instant chat and blogging. As the year 2000 passed, about 100 million individuals had internet connections. Social networking, on the other hand, was seen as an uncommon pastime at the time. Nonetheless, individuals from all over the world began to use chat rooms to meet new people, date, and debate subjects with others who shared their interests. The massive social media explosion, on the other hand, had yet to come. These are just a few of the platforms that people use nowadays. Part of the appeal is that there is literally something for everyone. But there's more to it than that—a set of traits that bind the entire notion together.

Social media has grown so ingrained in urbanites' everyday lives that it's difficult to fathom a day—let alone a week—without it. Even though some of us go on a "social media detox" every now and then or try to avoid it entirely, there's no disputing its development and effect on your lifestyles. Social media platforms are no longer limited to—even if they are dominated by—certain groups, from young to old, people to companies. For most of you, it's a source of information, a way to connect with others, a place to express yourselves, or even a call to action; for others, it's their bread and butter. According to survey report, 3.88 billion individuals were using social media in 2021. Although Google tops the most-visited sites rankings, social networking sites account for a significant portion of internet users' online time. This data illustrates that social media marketing should be a part of any marketer's plan.

Businesses cannot afford to ignore social media because it provides far too many opportunities to engage with customers.

Are you ready to make a new start?

Sometimes you choose to reinvent yourselves, but most of the time you are compelled to do so owing to a layoff, a major life event, or even a worldwide pandemic. While you have little control over such circumstances, you can choose how you respond in the future and utilise them to propel yourselves into a better, more satisfying future. Working in the city and travelling globally was my ideal job as a leader. In certain circumstances, your existing and desired brands are quite similar. And if it all ended tomorrow, you'd be remembered exactly how you wanted to be remembered. A plan will help you remain on track by ensuring that your behavior and appearance online and in person are consistent, reinforcing your brand. Consistency, not perfection, is what you need to define your unique brand. It's all about where you are right now.

- What difficulties have you faced as a result of your reputation?
- Have you encountered any roadblocks that require a strategy to overcome?
- Are you doomed or attractive in the digital world?

First impressions are becoming increasingly rare in today's world. People check you out in the virtual world before they engage with you in the real world. Someone may be searching for you on the internet right now, seconds before a meeting with you. Your internet reputation will have an influence on your success. Digital is critical if you want to expand your strategic network or promote yourself.

The world of social media is a busy place. You must make an impression.

With a personal brand, you can send a consistent message across all of your social media sites and pages. You'll go over the main social networking networks in this book and figure out which one is best for you. You'll also design profiles and pages that emphasise your skills while speaking to your potential customers. You'll then go through how to develop engaging material and keep track of your progress. You'll also go through how to target your audience and when to spend money on advertisements. Finally, I'll demonstrate how to post to a variety of social networking platforms. Please don't get too worked up. The procedure is broken down into simple steps in this course. You have a lot of work ahead of you.

As technology advances, accessibility will increasingly be at the centre of discussions about careers, as well as job growth and networking. Using social media and having some sort of digital presence is essential for professional growth and development. Can you elaborate on the function that has had over time and how you've watched it take shape? So you're fascinated by societal change, particularly as it relates to professional branding? When you first started, social media was simply like Myspace, and Facebook was just starting to take off. But then it evolved into a digital environment that allowed you to show others who you really are. But it eventually evolved into a digital environment that enabled you to show others exactly who you were, who you are, and who you aspire to be. And it's simply been amazing to be able to affect so much over time. right? Companies are increasingly looking at your social media presence first to get a sense of who you are.

It's not just LinkedIn either. LinkedIn, Facebook, Instagram, Twitter, your websites, and blogs, to name a few. So, in my opinion, it's critical for people to lean in to what they want that story to be rather than control it. so that others are aware of who you are and what you stand for. It's critical to maintain all of those things current and new because people are always on the lookout for them, and look how you ended up connecting and finding one another. It's a direct result of it. Is that correct? So your resume isn't the only thing that speaks for you, and in that way, a lot of these digital ecosystems, these social ecosystems, are allowing them to speak for you before you ever meet someone.

Take a minute to consider what you actually need to express to the audiences you're attempting to reach at this point in time. Changing forces sales pitches to be more sympathetic and timely. So, looking at the entire landscape, understanding that, but also understanding that, going back to my love for social media and kind of what my role is, social media immediately became the place where everyone went to, not only to get the news, but also to find a level of escapism into just being, whether it was through entertainment and TikTok, hashtag challenges and things like that, or to find some new cooking opportunity, you know, because there was that downtime.

I worked with a diverse range of clients, including established and emerging business executives, entrepreneurs, high-potential employees, job seekers, college students, and anyone else seeking more control and intention in their career. Personal branding allows you the chance to take a step back, pause where you are, and ask yourself, "Where do I want to be ?" It doesn't always imply you're in transition. So, when it comes to the personal branding process, I prefer to think of it as taking the randomness out of your job and allowing you to create a game plan and strategy that will help you make wise decisions. So, if you imagine five years ahead:

- Who do you want to be in five years?
- What are your interests and passions?
- Who motivates you?
- What are some of your abilities and talents that you'd like to develop?

If you're more of a creative type and want to attract the attention of ad directors or marketing agencies, Instagram could be a better fit for you. It's critical to consider where your audience is when you're establishing your internet presence and brand. And, of course, let your online audience know how they can assist you; use the real estate you have on all of these sites to promote your brand and inform people about what you do. Is your Facebook timeline photo of a sunset or a snapshot of your dog, for example? You may use a photo of yourself speaking in front of a huge gathering to help your friends remember who you are.

Personal branding is the most effective technique to reach a wider audience and develop a worldwide image.

Perhaps you're looking for a new career, a promotion, or some more tools and resources in your current position. It's quite tough to favorably influence individuals who are making judgments about whether or not to give you that job or those resources if you don't have a clear and powerful value proposition, a personal brand. Your target audience is the individuals who have those opportunities, and you need to be in the right place for them. You can create influence when you know what your value offer is, who your target audience is, and what your goals are.

If you're a nice, approachable professional, let your tone, pictures, and materials reflect that. If, on the other hand, you're trying to establish a more exclusive, reserved brand stance, you'll want to avoid being too informal or talkative with your online acquaintances. It's critical to interact and participate in the conversation as if you were in a real-life situation. The same thing happens on the internet. If someone sends you a message or shares something that interests you, answer and express your thoughts. Your personal brand provides you with direction and purpose. It takes the guesswork out of how you'll present yourself, the relationships you'll form, and where you'll go in your career. It's all about you when it comes to personal branding. While there are formulae and measurements to follow, your route is yours alone, and you must have faith in your ideals to make this work. Begin by taking stock of your existing brand. Accept and comprehend it rather than judging it, but devise a strategy and implement it. Use your personal brand to assist you make important decisions, such as which firm to work for, what outfit makes you feel the most confident, and what your blog's banner should be.

Can you honestly answer the question of how you got here when you consider your career and where you are now? Did you create it yourself or was it created for you? You accepted jobs because someone believed you'd be excellent at something, or because they gave you more money or more pleasure, and you went in that way. You didn't plan anything ahead of time. What would five people who know you say about you if you asked them what they believe you're excellent at or what makes you unique? Would they respond to you in the same way that you might respond to yourself? Personal branding gives your reputation purpose and emphasis, ensuring that others view you the way you want them to. What if I told you that your capacity to create and maintain influence is precisely proportional to your professional power? A powerful and appealing personal brand is necessary for gaining influence. So, what exactly is a brand? A brand, on the other hand, is an expectation of an experience.

As a result, personal branding provides you with that sensation of power, but keep in mind that it's always about the emotional side of things. Personal branding is how people see you, and it provides you with the feeling of purpose and strategy that you need to make decisions as you advance in your profession. Just because you can doesn't mean you should, as I like to say. It's also worth noting that just because you want to doesn't imply you can. So, taking stock of where you are and what you want to achieve with your career, as well as what it might take to get there, is something you'll go over in depth in this course. And you'll discover that you can go from a reactive to a proactive job, something that's much more intentional and much more proactive.

It's critical to making a good first impression. Being real, on the other hand, requires knowing what's suitable and mastering the art of self-editing. Self-editing implies that you are aware of your approach, and that you are aware of when you may be truthful and honest and when you must withhold judgment. It's all about being authentic. It's always about your values to know what's in your heart and what's directing your plan. Take note of how your hands are positioned. Make sure you're not pointing at someone or being excessively directive if you're talking with your hands. Make a welcome gesture with your hands to demonstrate approachability. Show that you're open to new ideas and inviting them by raising your hands. Though your fists are closed or your hands are clasped, it may appear as if you are extremely tight, making you appear unapproachable. Take note of your posture as well. I've never met anybody whose personal brand was supposed to be locked off and unapproachable. As a result, when you go into a room, have your shoulders back and your posture confident and friendly.

Are you doomed or attractive in the digital world?

First impressions are becoming increasingly rare in today's world. People check you out in the virtual world before they engage with you in the real world. Someone may be searching for you on the internet right now, seconds before a meeting with you. Your internet reputation will have an influence on your success. Digital is critical if you want to expand your strategic network or promote yourself. Now, I get what you're thinking: if I want to advance internally, why do I need an internet brand? When it comes to your firm, even your own employees are checking you out on the internet. And they're basing their judgments on what Google says about you. Have you ever utilised Google to look up people in your own company? Having a strong digital presence might help demonstrate to decision-makers that you're up to date on technology. Your internet presence might set you apart from your colleagues and persuade others that your promotion is deserving. Digital technology may be perplexing and daunting to many of us. For some of you, even the mention of social media is enough to make you shut down. You're committed to eradicating digital anxiety and replacing it with a strong online presence.

Keep in mind that each platform is distinct. LinkedIn, for example, is a professional networking site. You want to join groups in your sector, or perhaps the target industry you want to go into, and you want to post on LinkedIn on a regular basis. When you upload articles or links, share your thoughts on them. What do you think of my point of view? Professionals, recruiters, hiring managers, and thought leaders all utilise LinkedIn, which is a strong and widely used platform.

As a result, make sure your personal brand is consistent with what I'll see when I meet you in person. On the other hand, Facebook is a more sociable network. It enables you to humanise your company's image.In my situation, I'm linked on Facebook to a lot of my clients, individuals who have read my books or heard me speak, and the media. As a result, I always make sure the message is free of errors and unsuitable information, but I do let them see my sociable side. It completes my own branding plan. Now is a wonderful time to consider or review your online profiles. Are they compatible? Do they appear to be consistent?

What do you believe people think of you? It's an important aspect of personal branding.

Everyone nowadays is aware of and uses social media. Even the most distant regions of the globe are aware of Facebook and Twitter, and many of them use them on a daily basis. It wasn't like this a decade ago, though. At the time, not many individuals had access to the internet, and cellphones were yet to be introduced to the market. Most of us now can't imagine your lives without social media. You check Facebook, Twitter, Instagram, and Pinterest at least three times every hour. The capacity to utilise the internet to share and interact with others virtually quickly is how most people define social media. According to this concept, social media can be traced down to a single website—no, it isn't Facebook.

There are numerous types of social media.There's vanilla Facebook, bite-sized dessert Twitter, and a dish with the ideal presentation. Pinterest, on-the-go Instagram, and, of course, zero-calorie Snapchat. The word "free" has a lot of power. People will try something for free right away, which is why these platforms are so popular. They provide all of these incredible capabilities and connections without the need to pay for them. The platform's secret sauce is in the advertising charges and paid games, but the entry fee is zero.

It's not about who you are when it comes to your personal brand. It all boils down to who you are. And that's why planning is so crucial, because your personal brand isn't defined by your uniform, job title, credentials, or résumé. Your personal brand communicates to your target audience who you are, what you believe in, and how you can add value to their lives. Some people are drawn to personal branding because it is a difficult task. Perhaps you've completed the activities in the previous movies and noticed that your existing brand is present but your ideal brand is not. There's a tremendous difference between who you are now and how you want to be recognised. You'll need a plan to fill that in.

What exactly does success entail for you?

You must see yourself in that moment a year from now, along with all the consequences. all of the advantages. The joy you feel, the satisfaction you get, and the people in your life who are rooting for you and cheering you on. The sky is the limit when it comes to your friends, loved ones, and family. Now put all of your efforts towards achieving that objective. Personal branding is what it is, and it will help you stand out. Opportunities may present themselves as a result of others talking about your great efforts. People are drawn to those who give back. The finest personal brands, the best leaders, are frequently perceived as compassionate, resourceful, and giving back for a reason. Because being a connection is what helps your society thrive, you're having a positive influence on society. To sum up, always consider how you may be a connection rather than a networker. Consider how you might link opportunities with people and causes. I'm not advising you to live like the Godfather, but if you can connect dots, uncover opportunities, and do it in a selfless manner without expecting anything in return, you've developed one of the greatest talents of personal brand leaders, which is the ability to connect. This is not the same as being a typical networker. A networker, in my opinion, is motivated by the ability to find something that is both good for others and profitable for themselves. A connector is a person who seeks out opportunities for people in their surroundings.

Opportunities may present themselves as a result of others talking about your great efforts.

Personal Branding Success Stories while your personal brand may be in its infancy, there are several examples of great personal branding available today. Look to these experts for guidance and inspiration. Branding comes effortlessly after you know who you want to be.

" Bad luck either destroys you or makes you the man or woman you really are." -Amitabh Bachchan

Like every other Power Brand, whether it's Coke, Google, or Facebook, Amitabh's career in Bollywood began with the film "Saat Hindustani." And, in the same way that Coke has become associated with happiness, Google has become a'verb,' and Facebook has grown into a 'alternative universe,' with billions of users, Amitabh Bachchan has evolved and is now known as 'Is sadi ka Maha Nayak.' Brand building takes time, whether it's for an enterprise or an individual. A Power Brand is the result of years of effort, with a fair number of successes, failures, and setbacks, as well as significant comebacks, all following a consistent procedure. The brand becomes more relevant and effective when it is approached from a value-driven perspective. The brand's effect is maintained through being present across different media platforms. The credibility of a brand is enhanced by its journey, which is supported by appropriate performance and recognition. And you can see it all in the way Amitabh Bachchan's personal brand has grown in leaps and bounds. The trajectory of this brand shows a defined strategic route and direction.

" Frankly I've never really subscribe to these adjectives tagging me as an icon, superstar, etc. I've always thought of myself as an actor doing his job to the best of his ability."- Amitabh Bachchan.

On your marketing collateral or resume, platitudes like cutting edge, state of the art, best services, outstanding customer experience, proven expertise, team-player, go-getter, seasoned professional, self-motivated, result-driven, problem solver, etc. make you sound like a choir rather than a unique, mesmerising voice. Big B made history as the first actor to appear on television with the famous Kaun Banega Crorepati program. From the super-hit angry young man of mainstream movies to the sartorially exquisite and well-informed presenter of an idiot box quiz show, he was an immediate success with the public once more. The lesson here is to search for unexpected possibilities to disrupt and innovate before others disrupt you, rather than continuing to travel solely the "safe" road.

He was also one of the first Bollywood stars to embrace social media, using Facebook and Twitter to interact with his fans. He even has a blog! Leading brands of the past are frequently threatened by extinction due to out-of-date regulations, out-of-date products, out-of-date marketing techniques, and a lackluster internet or social media presence. For those unfamiliar with Hindi, Big B's character wanders from rural to urban areas in search of work, and in this snippet, he introduces himself and displays his ability to speak English when the interviewer asks him to. And then there's 79-year-old Amitabh Bachchan, who recognised the new area and has begun to capitalise on his persona and famous position through assets that are digitally present in tokenised form, with restricted ownership and so avoiding the potential for duplication.

He has been the 'Shahenshah' throughout history, from the days of restricted media to the present day of ever-expanding media and ever-intruding social media. He's done it all and reigned supreme. With such ease, he has defied the prejudices associated with old age. With his cool quips, cool wardrobe, and coolest 'buddha hoga tera baap' image, Bachchan has managed to inspire all generations, because he doesn't seem to age. You all live in a world that is branded. Every product, from 'roti kapda aur makaan' to water, is on a branding journey. So, why should you continue to be commodities? You all need to work on developing your personal brands. There are several instances to learn from and be inspired by all around us. Amitabh Bachchan was able to achieve it because he refused to be limited by the constraints of a commodity-like existence. He is today's most powerful personality brand because he did not follow a predetermined route, but instead had the courage to venture into uncharted terrain. He achieved the pinnacle of success by changing the game's rules in the most relevant way.

" Change is the nature of life but challenges is the future of life. So challenges the changes. Never change the challenges." -Amitabh Bachchan

Celebrities are the greatest at busting the misconception that brand management is all about logos, colors, and marketing collateral. Especially those in the film industry. How did they become such iconic brands without using any of the standard branding tools? So much so that they started endorsing huge consumer companies with their personal brands. Amitabh Bachchan is a Bollywood actor. (For those unfamiliar with Indian cinema, Amitabh Bachchan, sometimes known as Big B, is the most popular actor in the country.) So, what makes him such a household name? What makes him such a timeless brand is a fascinating topic. It's difficult to think of another example of a brand with such broad appeal that spans decades. If it's just appearances, there are a plethora of performers that look as good as or better than him. If it comes to performance, there are a slew of them who are on par with or better than them.

Until the early 1970s, Bollywood was dominated by romance and romcoms, with established celebrities leading the business (notably among them, Rajesh Khanna, an actor par excellence). Big B shattered this with his angry-young-man persona in the film Zanjeer, and Bollywood cinema was never the same after that. Big B developed an unbreakable brand with his devotion and hard work after establishing himself as the new superstar. He is known for rehearsing his role, and you can see how well he coordinates everything, bringing the house down with each performance. He appears to have a firm grasp on the audience's pulse and is aware of what makes them tick. Everything is perfectly synchronized, from stance to gesture to dialog delivery to facial expression, culminating in that flawless execution that makes us laugh, weep, feel enraged, and so on.

"I am not a perfectionist, but I like to feel that things are done well. More important than that, I feel an endless need to learn, to improve, to evolve, not only to please the coach and the fans, but also to feel satisfied with myself. It is my conviction that here are no limits to learning, and that it can never stop, no matter what our age."—
Cristiano Ronaldo

Football slots provide players with the chance to win big as their hero, Cristiano Ronaldo, is prominently featured.

Ronaldo is no stranger to the gambling world; he has endorsed online casinos, so his appearance on a slot machine was only logical. He has his own brand, CR7, in addition to assisting other companies by providing endorsements. This business, named after the guy himself, began as a line of underwear but has now evolved into a variety of categories, including footwear, athletics, and socks. Cristiano and his company have a massive internet following of over 64 million followers on Twitter alone. But what goods has Cristiano Ronaldo worked on, and what else does he have planned? You'd be here all day if you listed all of Ronaldo's endorsements.

However, Nike is without a doubt the most important – and in terms of sports players, it's the world's largest sponsorship agreement, at an estimated $1 billion. He also took over as Armani's endorser from David Beckham, and he became a brand ambassador for Castrol (paid £8.2 million for the first two years, then £5.5 million after that) and Tag Heuer. KFC, Coca-Cola, and Emirates Airlines are among the other sponsors. Furthermore, with the popularity of casino slot games on the rise, it seemed only natural that he get engaged in this field as well. Cristiano Ronaldo rose to prominence after signing for Manchester United at the age of 18 in 2003. United won the FA Cup in his first season, then went on to win the Premier League three years in a row, the FIFA Club World Cup, and the UEFA Champions League. He's now one of the most well-known athletes in the world, and he's made the most of it. He's gone as far as establishing his own brand items after endorsing a variety of companies and earning a lot of money through sponsorship. The Cristiano Ronaldo brand is now valued at $8,000,000 by Forbes, making it one of the most expensive sports brands in the world.

> *"I see football as an art and all players are artists.*
> *If you are a top artist, the last thing you would do is paint a*
> *picture somebody else has already painted."*
> — *Cristiano Ronaldo*

Popular scientist Bill Nye is an excellent example of personal branding success. Since his television debut, Bill Nye has been renowned as the dad-joke-cracking, science-loving, global warming enthusiast that he is. Bill Nye demonstrates who he is and what he values to the audience by wearing a lab coat on his program and having an internet website dedicated to science-based material.

Kim Garst is a marketer who excels in social selling. Her business hinges around her personal image, which she isn't afraid to flaunt. Her social media platforms have a distinct presence, which adds to the evidence of her social marketing skills.

Tony Robbins is a motivational speaker. Tony Robbins is a divisive character, yet even if you dislike him, you are familiar with his name. Robbins, who is known for his self-help books and seminars, has always embodied his brand, from his energy to his personality to his beautiful teeth. Robbins' brand and public image exude confidence, pizzaz, and strength, as seen by his branding and public persona. Using social media to improve your personal branding personal branding is more crucial than ever in the age of social media and internet recruiting.

Oprah who? is a question you will never hear. You don't have to ask for a family name, you don't have to wonder who she is, and you don't have to act as if you know who she is, because you all do. Oprah Winfrey is a one-name behemoth, a global icon, the richest African-American of the twentieth century, and the biggest black philanthropist in American history. The Oprah Winfrey Show, an Academy Award nomination, $51 million donated to charity, and names, names, names of people she interviewed, mentored, elevated, affected, and helped. Several things come to mind when you hear the name Oprah Winfrey: her "favorite things," her book club, and, most significantly, her openness and empathy. That's because Oprah has mastered the art of personal branding. She's worked hard to change people's perceptions of her and to create good connotations with her name. The power of an empathy-based brand- when done correctly, your brand and personality are one and the same. She doesn't want to be branded, and this is now a part of her own brand. The technique of branding is thought to have originated with the ancient Egyptians, who used a unique sign burnt into the animal's skin with a hot branding iron to distinguish one person's cattle from another's. If any of the livestock were stolen, anybody who saw the emblem might figure out who owned them.

You are drawn to people who share your interests, and you gravitate toward people who understand you. It's not about being upbeat or seeming to be upbeat; it's about being understood. This is what you demand from companies and individuals. Consumers, not brands, are what people buy at the end of the day. This is why personal branding is so crucial, regardless of whether you call it that. You can't, however, feign it. It needs to be you in person. Oprah has been crowned the most influential woman of her generation by Life magazine. She was dubbed the greatest African-American philanthropist in American history by Business Week. With a net worth of $3 billion, she is one of the most successful entrepreneurs of all time. Oprah was born into a low-income family to an unmarried adolescent mother. She was sexually molested as a youngster and grew up to be a disturbed and rebellious adolescent. At the age of 13, she ran away from home. Despite her traumatic background, Oprah has refused to let her past define her future. She illustrated that no matter what challenges you confront, with passion, commitment, and hard work, you can achieve anything.

"We all have our imperfections. But I'm human, and you know, it's important to concentrate on other qualities besides outer beauty."-Beyonce

Beyonce Knowles the entrepreneur and music superstar. It's no coincidence that pop singer Beyoncé has developed a massive worldwide brand. She's one of the most prominent performers in the entertainment world, and she's been named one of Time Magazine's top 100 Most Influential People in the World on many occasions. She has a net worth of at least $355 million and has earned several honors and accolades as one of the best-selling music artists of all time. Not only that, but Beyoncé is a businessman and entrepreneur who has developed a massive worldwide brand.

"I don't feel like I have to please anyone. I feel free. I feel like I'm an adult. I'm grown. I can do what I want. I can say what I want. I can retire if I want. That's why I've worked hard."- Beyonce

What is it that you believe in and would fight for?

The self-evaluation Doing a brutally honest, true self-assessment is one of the most crucial things you can do in order to discover your superpower and your most authentic best self. It destroyes the entire idea if you aren't honest. You're attempting to get to the heart of who you are and what you want to achieve. As a result, it's critical to be nice to yourself while still being honest with yourself. Whatever the challenge or opportunity in front of you, the ultimate end result and purpose of what you're doing here is to be able to cast light on the route to the good work that is required in the world today. Then there's the question of how you're presenting yourself. How are you acting in a way that reflects those values? It's similar to the "walk the talk" concept. You must be able to tell people what you believe in and then follow through with action. That is how credit is obtained. That is how credibility is gained.

- What is the best way for us to remember you?
- What impression did you leave on others?
- Are they joyful and celebrating your life because they were glad to meet you?
- Are you asking yourselves, "What did you stand for?"
- What do you want people to think of you when you're gone?

The power of this practice, as unpleasant as it is, is that it allows you to reclaim control. You get to tilt the lens backwards and re-engineer from this day to that day if you can think about the end, the literal end of your existence. And while it may be a long way off, you have the opportunity to consider how you want to live today, tomorrow, and the following day in order to achieve the reputation you seek. Every action you do, every friendship you form, every decision you make, and every business decision you make will help you achieve the reputation you desire at the end of your life. That, as unpleasant as it is, is the exercise's power. It provides you with options and control. Close your eyes and imagine what you want people to remember and feel about you at the end of your life.

It might be an opportunity to join a new project, manage a team, get a promotion, or even a springboard for landing a new career or starting your own business. Begin by keeping your eyes out for opportunities to exhibit your abilities in other areas. You should try to boost your visibility in areas where you don't have a strong reputation. Talk to folks on different teams, describe your aim, and ask where they think you'd be a good fit. After that, focus on preserving your reputation. Politics in any workplace may be complicated, so you need to keep reaffirming and safeguarding your brand's value. This is accomplished by gently correcting anyone who misunderstands your worth, avoiding workplace gossip, and never burning bridges.

How can you be expected to keep a tight lip as you advance in your career if you're eager to divulge information to a coworker? From here, share your vision with everyone who can assist you in achieving your objectives. You could discover unexpected sponsors among your coworkers, managers, or even individuals in positions of power at your firm. Share your greater ambitions with your manager; if you're lucky enough to have a supportive supervisor, they'll want to assist you in achieving your goals. Finally, brag about your achievements. I understand how difficult it is to handle self-promotion at work, but it is essential.

You frequently undervalue the instruments at your disposal for influencing others. To exert influence, you must first determine which currencies are available. Currencies are items that you give to others and that others value. You have two types of currencies to choose from. The first is tangible currency, which includes items like pay raises, extra yearly leave, and promotions. These are obviously powerful, but you seldom, if ever, get access to them, especially on a daily basis. The key thing to keep in mind is that you do have choices. When you're trying to influence someone, it might be intimidating, especially if the stakeholder is senior or you don't have control over them.

When you don't have control over the stakeholders, all you have to do is do a far better job of understanding the currencies that could be relevant and acceptable. Then you need to be systematic in how you communicate your needs so that the other person sees the benefit of working with you. There are, on the other hand, soft currencies, and there are a lot more of them. These might include things like networking, building partnerships, establishing a common goal, increasing exposure, and so on. The main thing to remember about soft currencies is that you don't have to be a senior executive or have a lot of expertise to use them effectively. Consider yourself working on a project that requires assistance, and you're attempting to persuade people to assist you. If one of the benefits of the project is that you'll be able to show the results to top company stakeholders, this might be a great opportunity for someone looking to advance and get exposure.

This is why it's critical to first learn about the values of the person you're attempting to persuade. If someone isn't interested in enhancing their own awareness, the cash you suggested might be worthless.

I'd like you to spend some time making a list of all the currencies you have. The first is for firm while the second is for soft. Regardless of your position within the firm, the list of soft currencies is likely to be far longer than the list of hard currencies after you complete this exercise. Not all currencies will function, and others may only work in certain situations. It's easy to get wordy and spend too much time telling a narrative, but if you hold your audience's attention by focusing on the few crucial things that matter, you'll keep their interest. Furthermore, anyone who wishes to learn more can do so. So keep it brief and to the point. Write a 15-second and 30-second rendition of your tale, akin to an elevator pitch. You should be able to quickly tell your brand narrative in a way that makes you distinctive and leaves a positive impact. Finally, offer your narrative to someone you can trust for criticism and suggestions. Use that information to boost your confidence and go where you want to go.

It is natural to cling to the past. You cling to what you know because it is familiar and secure. As you begin to rethink all of the many elements of yourselves and your lives, what no longer serves you or fits with who you want to be, it's common to experience some sort of identity crisis as you begin to reevaluate all of the different aspects of yourselves and your lives. Apple challenged the globe to "Think Different." Nike pushed individuals to "Just Do It," regardless of their age, gender, or degree of physical condition. "America Runs on Dunkin'," Dunkin' Donuts convinced busy professionals. These well-known phrases have evolved into rallying cries through time, establishing the tone for how each brand communicates and defines itself in the marketplace. These slogans have communicated a narrative and changed how people see the organizations behind them in only a few words. They show the power and promise of branding when viewed as a whole.

A powerful brand stands out from the crowd, resulting in greater sales, enhanced awareness, and improved customer experiences. However, branding isn't just for businesses. Professionals each have their own narrative to tell, as well as their unique set of aspirations, abilities, and knowledge. A personal brand is no more a nice-to-have in today's increasingly digital world; it's expected. Your narrative has the potential to help you launch or advance your career. In fact, 85% of hiring managers say that a job candidate's personal brand has an impact on their recruiting decisions. Your personal brand should emphasise your talents, develop a reputation, foster trust, and explain the distinct qualities you contribute to your current (or desired) industry. Your personal brand, if well-cultivated, will indicate to employers whether or not you'll be a good fit for an available position. If you're wanting to change occupations or break into a new industry, personal branding is critical.

Your personal brand is both your most valuable asset and the most effective marketing instrument you can employ. You crave a more personal connection as your world becomes more technologically linked, and you gravitate toward firms that have a face behind the brand. With the rise and effect of influencer marketing on social media, you can see the shift. Why is influencer marketing so successful in the corporate world? because it humanises a commercial by providing a tale about a real person going through real life. But they aren't just any influencers. They're business owners who have built strong personal brands and devoted fan bases. It makes no difference what sort of business you're in. Understanding personal branding may help you advance in your job or business.

Who are your current clients, and why did they choose to do business with you? See where the common thread is by looking for shared pain areas, features, and hobbies. Have you discovered any trends or key words as a result of working with these clients that you can use to improve your service descriptions or marketing messaging? It's extremely probable that your product or service will help others who are similar to them. The second suggestion is to know all there is to know about your product or service. Choose precise demographics to target since greater clarity leads to more conversions. Age, location, gender, income, education level, marriage or family status, and employment are all things to consider. Take into account the psychographics, or the more personal attributes, of an ideal candidate.

Your brand is your public identity, what you're trusted for. And for your brand to endure, it has to be tested, redefined, managed, and expanded as markets evolve. Brands either learn or disappear.

If you're seeking work, your web presence may make or break your chances. Given that the typical employment duration is roughly four years, you'll almost certainly be looking for work at some point, so start working on your personal brand now. With that in mind, let's look at how you may start developing a strong personal brand. Leveraging your differences is crucial for brand development. Your own brand won't be genuinely personal if you're just like everyone else. Those who stand out are remembered. That's where your one-of-a-kind value proposition comes in. It's a brief sentence that summarises what you provide that no one else does. When it comes to establishing your distinct value proposition, you should follow these two steps: Identify your advantages. Consider where you've previously excelled. Consider what people say about you and what they think your skills are.

The cornerstone of your distinct value proposition is determining what you do better than most others. Building a personal brand from the bottom up does not happen quickly, and it may be stressful. Here are questions to ask yourself to help you get organised and learn more about how to further develop your personal brand. Before you get started, keep in mind that your personal brand is an expression of who you are and what you believe in. It's what sets you apart from the competitors, and it's something no one can take away from you. Therefore, it's critical to examine yourself. That takes me to the first question you'll have to respond to. What is it that you am enthusiastic about? Your personal brand should always have a central emphasis on which you are really enthusiastic.

You must identify both personal and professional hobbies, as your personal brand should be a mix of your present competence and real-life tales and lessons. There is no quick fix for establishing a powerful personal brand. It takes a lot of effort, perseverance, and patience, so it's great if you're enthusiastic about the adventure. The second issue to consider is, "What do I excel at?" When establishing the foundation of your personal brand, make sure to emphasize your strengths. Are you a terrific public speaker, a brilliant writer, or a fantastic photographer, for example?

Don't strive to be someone you know you're good at, and define what you know you're good at. Making the most of your abilities and skills while serving your ideal client should be a goal for your personal brand. This permits you to enjoy your business while also putting your customers in a better position than before you met them. Examining your LinkedIn profile is one way to acquire insight into your skills. Create accounts and sites that emphasize your expertise to get the most out of social media. Your knowledge should be prominent and consistent across all social media platforms. The first step is to select three areas of competence by looking through your personal brand statement, offers, and brand purpose. Once you've written down your top qualities, competencies you can use at least two ways you can use each of your top characteristics to make a substantial contribution to your professional network. Everyone wants to present themselves in the best light possible. You could assume that this signifies that you aren't good enough right now. Expecting yourself to be flawless just adds to your sense of inadequacy, and you risk disappointing people by setting unreasonable goals for yourself that you can't possibly accomplish.

How to use social media effectively?

Many individuals believe it is a mistake to "give it all away" with free material. Why would someone hire or pay you if you give everything away? It's the polar opposite. Providing free, useful content demonstrates that you know what you're talking about. It demonstrates your knowledge. Imagine what you would do if the free advice worked. As a result, the first step is to make all of the information you publish truly useful and informative. You want to be known as a credible expert in your field. Step two is to conduct some research on what topics in your area are creating interest. Google Keyword Planner, Google Trends, and Exploding Topics are all excellent tools for discovering what's hot. You can then proceed. By 2022, freelancers and contract employees will make up 47% of the total workforce. If this describes you, a personal brand can help you attract clients and earn more money. It aids in the establishment of your reliability and dependability, as well as allows clients to locate you.

Furthermore, according to a 2018 CareerBuilder poll, 70% of employers screen prospects by examining their social media, and 43% use it to check on current employees. If you're seeking work, your web presence may make or break your chances. Given that the typical employment duration is roughly four years, you'll almost certainly be looking for work at some point, so start working on your personal brand now. With that in mind, let's look at how you may start developing a strong personal brand. It's crucial to figure out this information if you want your personal brand to be an accurate picture of who you are, what talents you have, and what your goals are.

"A great brand is a story that's never completely told. A brand is a metaphorical story that connects with something very deep – a fundamental appreciation of mythology. Stories create the emotional context people need to locate themselves in a larger experience." – Scott Bedbury

While perseverance is a virtue, not all perseverants are extroverted, fun-loving, or likeable. These personality qualities, when paired with your skills, make you stand out from the crowd. It's most likely a unique blend that works well for you. Sometime around late 2019 or early 2020,

LinkedIn became a true "social" media network, rather than merely a copy of your résumé. LinkedIn unveiled a slew of new features in 2021, including a "creator" mode for influencers (and aspiring influencers) on the network. It's more difficult to get into the Twittersphere and establish yourself as a legitimate influencer, but you may employ comparable strategies as you would on LinkedIn.

Follow thought leaders in your preferred field, leave smart comments on their articles, retweet them, and start tweeting your own insightful opinions. Wherever possible, use pertinent hashtags. The key to success on Twitter, like any other site, is consistency. The more meaningful discussions you have with people in your specialty, the more likely you are to be successful.

Sharing a range of material across numerous channels improves your visibility and speeds up the development of your brand. While it may not be possible to cover all forms of information, try not to limit yourself to just one or two. Rather, attempt to rotate through at least four or five of these content kinds and post them on different channels. Although it was briefly stated in the previous section, now is the time to stress the necessity of providing value to your audience. Making stale content is simple, but creating information that is intelligent, engaging, and actually helpful to your readers is a different matter.

Planning and intention are required when creating good material. "Would this benefit me?" ask yourself when you plan your materials. "Can this be done?" Don't accept nonsense or cliched counsel. Make material that will have a significant impact on your audience's lives. Finally, while having a large following may appear impressive, it means nothing if no one interacts with you. Building a community means providing an environment where people can communicate with one another, get to know one another, and assist one another. This is a wonderful method to set yourself apart if you're seeking new business. This also helps if you just want to get your name out there to enhance your profession.

> *"People do not buy goods and services. They buy relations, stories and magic." – Seth Godin*

Ask yourself the following questions:

- What makes me tick?
- What skills do I possess?
- What tasks sap my energy? What kind of job motivates me?
- In what environments do I work best?
- What industries pique my interest?
- What do I want to be when I'm done with my career?
- What kind of influence do I want to have?

It's fine if the answers to these questions alter over time. Because your personal brand changes along with you, it's vital that you be honest today and understand that your image may change in the future. In an age where harsh behavior, especially by famous personalities, appears almost acceptable, I declare that the golden rule of treating others as you would want them to treat you is still the best way to maintain your integrity and personal brand.

Make sure you ask the proper questions. Find out how having a fresh candidate in place will assist the interviewer if you're seeking a job or promotion. What would the interviewer be able to accomplish as a result? If a potential supervisor, team member, or coworker mentions a goal they want the new recruit to achieve, inquire as to why it is so essential. What difference will it make in their lives? The answers to these critical questions will help you define your value offer. Here's a brief illustration: It's now your turn. Consider something you do on a daily basis at work. What is the importance of your job to your team or organization? Respect people if you want to be respected. It's important to share what you've learned. Be present for your friends and family when they need you. Unconditionally love and enjoy life without remorse. That statement is reflected in all you do. It assists you in maintaining my personal and professional brand integrity.

"For a truly effective social campaign, a brand needs to embrace the first principles of marketing, which involves brand definition and consistent storytelling." – Simon Mainwaring

I will provide both strategic insight and practical ideas for building and managing a brand in this book by expanding your professional network by stepping outside of your comfort zone, using social media to communicate and collaborate. Imagine being able to make money from your passions. Getting paid to do what you love is a dream come true. Obtaining the greatest tools, cutting-edge innovations, and game-changing goods in your field all while increasing the size of your bank account day by day.

Continuous education allows you to reach new career milestones and realize your ambitions. Returning the favors you've been given and winning graciously while maintaining your integrity to repair any brand harm that has occurred. Leading with the ultimate objective of service in mind and mentoring others is a gratifying experience for both the mentor and the mentee. LinkedIn is the most widely used networking platform for business professionals and job seekers throughout the world. This is due to the fact that it accentuates what you know by forming relationships with the appropriate individuals. You'll discover how to uncover new chances, build your personal brand, network with other professionals, massively advance your career, and obtain your ideal job in LinkedIn personal branding and marketing secrets. You'll be able to find your ideal job and build your business in no time if you follow the methods in the book. Will you be able to dominate your competitors and drive massive amounts of traffic to your content without paying for it? the next influencer whose identity is inextricably linked to the immense value you bring to customers?

If you're not sure how to respond to these queries, seek advice from friends, coworkers, and family. Even if you're certain of your answers, it's a good idea to get advice from others. They perceive you in a way that you don't see yourself, and this might help you develop a more complete picture of yourself. Once you've become conscious of these many aspects of yourself, you can start creating an image that corresponds to them and helps you achieve where you want to go.This also attracts like-minded folks who share your motivations or recognize value in what you have to give. This strengthens the network.

You may create your brand around your strengths by taking stock of them. Share your knowledge and accomplishments with others. All of this develops credibility and trust, so if an employer is considering you or you're searching for a customer, they'll be able to determine from your brand that you're the ideal person for the job. If you've identified your skills but aren't sure how to transform them into a value proposition, consider how you would prepare for an interview. Here are some ideas for figuring out what makes you unique: Make sure your response is detailed. Many people are dedicated workers who pay attention to detail and get along with others. Consider concrete examples of when your hard work or people skills paid dividends. What characteristics of yourself contributed to the success of such scenarios? What enabled you to achieve what you accomplished rather than others with similar abilities?

In Facebook and LinkedIn allow users to establish discussions on relevant subjects and converse with one another. You may chime in as many times as you like to start a discussion. It's difficult to exaggerate the importance of seeing people in person. You may have one-on-one meetings or host big groups of people to come together, discuss, and learn. You may use webinars to bring people together for a shared learning experience. This is an opportunity for you to get to know your audience, share your knowledge, and continue to grow as a person. While developing a personal brand takes time and effort, the benefits are immense when done effectively. Personal brands enable you to cultivate a network of experts who recognise your value and consider you first when new possibilities occur.

A personal brand may help you create revenue, advance your profession, find a mentor, or never have to seek for work again. Customers will follow you on social media to see what you're up to and how you can assist them. You could be missing out on valuable business and new leads if you don't have a strong social media presence. Here are a few simple methods to use social media to establish your own brand:

- Keep your social media profiles current and relevant.
- Use social scheduling apps to make it easier to post more frequently.

- Create material that will pique your audience's attention.
- Talk and share with your audience whenever possible.
- Join and participate in relevant online discussion forums.
- Maintain a consistent brand voice, tone, and image across all media channels.
- Import contacts from sales funnels and email lists.
- Make sure your material is upbeat.

You agree that career management is your responsibility, not your employer's. In terms of perspective, it challenges the notion that there is a limited set of important abilities and behaviors that must be mastered in order to be successful. And that, with the right help, any aspiring professional can master them. I feel that success is linked to the one-of-a-kind component that each of us has to contribute if you're prepared to be introspective and boldly be yourselves, your best selves, all of the time. There is no right or wrong response, but you must have your own unique perspective. If you don't, you're a commodity, doing the same thing as everyone else with the same job title. When you take a stance and express an opinion, you set yourself apart from the crowd.

Now, if it doesn't come to you right away, take some time to think about it. Allow your subconscious mind to work on it while following your blast sheet as a guide. It's time to move on to step three after you've determined your distinct thought leadership issue and strong point of view. You must show and share your enthusiasm for your field of expertise. That's how you establish yourself as the go-to man. You must demonstrate and inform. It's time to turn on the turbochargers. Let's start with some pointers on how to show and tell internally, or within your organization. Contribute to your company's intranet or publication with material. You can conduct training or a lunch-and-learn event. Helping people in your field of expertise may also be a form of reverse mentorship. When your issue comes up in meetings, speak up. Look for a project that requires your expertise and volunteer to help. Now let's look at your external network. Getting promoted faster is closely associated with gaining a reputation outside of your organization.

With over 200 million monthly active users, LinkedIn has the ability to take your personal brand to the next level. LinkedIn is an excellent resource for establishing industry authority and reputation. Include your contact information, a high-quality profile photo, a full bio, your career history, and customer testimonials or endorsements on your page to boost the chances of making new contacts. Underneath your photo, banner, title, and other basic information, your bio is the major block of text. Before clicking see more, viewers only see the first two lines of your bio, so make those two lines count. But, once you've met all of the prerequisites, what should you do next on LinkedIn? Provide your industry knowledge.

LinkedIn is all about making connections with individuals in your field. Take it a step further and strive to give crucial insights, takeaways, and your unique viewpoint on current news by writing and posting articles on top of covering major industry news and trends. Your published articles will appear in your activity section, and you should have at least three published pieces that speak to your industry experience and thoughts. As a consequence, your profile will appear more authentic, and more individuals will accept your connection requests. Tell your tale with the use of video. LinkedIn has officially opted to enter the video industry, which is the fastest growing trend on social media.

So, on your LinkedIn page, include films that reflect the story of you and your company. Show your LinkedIn friends some behind-the-scenes footage, an exclusive sneak peek of a new product release, or a soon-to-be-released project via video. Remember that when it comes to video, the options are unlimited. Pay attention to the people you're connected to. It's not just about the number of connections you build or the number of LinkedIn followers you have; it's about the number of individuals you reach and engage with. Consider the importance of good connections. The more like-minded your contacts are, the more likely your material will strike a chord with them, resulting in engagement and lead generation.

So, here are some pointers for externally exhibiting and telling. Make a presentation to a group of professionals. Join three LinkedIn groups that are relevant to your field of expertise and contribute to the discussion. Make a blog post or a blog post and share it on LinkedIn. Research Make a list of five thought leaders in your field and invite them to join your network. Bring together a group of people who are experts in your field, either in person or digitally, for a dynamic conversation. I hope the terms *"expert"* and "thought leader" have become less daunting to you. Each of you is passionate about something that can be developed. Each of you has a point of view. What you need now is a strategy for actively and extensively communicating your knowledge and point of view. Spend some time analyzing and strategizing on your blast sheet. And I challenge everyone of you to create a blog article or give a presentation about your specialized knowledge. Then you'll be good to go and ready to demonstrate and share. Once you start actively sharing, you'll come across as the one-of-a-kind professional you are: a go-to expert, a vital thought leader, ready to tackle the next problem at work, ready to contribute at a higher, more senior level, positioned and poised.

Why is it vital to establish a personal brand?

People are already making assumptions and judgments about who you are and what you stand for, even if you don't speak at conferences, have a social media presence, or generate content. The point is that you have a brand, whether you like it or not. Why not use that opportunity to take charge of your brand and help mold it to better represent your personality?

Pinterest is also a good place to visit. You might also type in "cake design" here. They'll make some suggestions here, and you should click on the ones they make. Perhaps jot down some of their suggestions in case you wish to apply them in the future. When you click on cake design, you'll notice a lot of stuff that could appeal to your ideal customer. You're going to move to Twitter now. On Twitter, you should start with a hashtag. I'm going to input cake design into this box. And here you'll find a collection of tweets featuring various types of cake designs or people. You should now have a good notion of the kind of material your audience consumes on a daily basis. Use this data to engage with your ideal customer and generate content that is relevant to them.

I'd want you to consider the following two questions. Do you know how others see you? What do people say about you when you mention your name? The answer is a bit of a mystery for most of you. You may believe you have a good reputation, or you may believe there is space for improvement. In any case, seeking input from others is an excellent first step toward developing your own brand. This is what I'd like you to do. Within your current close network, choose someone you can trust. Determine who you believe can supply you with open, honest, and straightforward feedback.

It might be a long-time friend, a former employer, or a coworker you have faith in. One wonderful approach is to get input from two different people: someone who has known you for a long time, at least two to three years, and someone you've just met. These two types of individuals will assist in providing a wider range of input. Take the time to meet with a trustworthy friend or family member and ask them these questions. What do most people think of you? In three words, I'd describe myself.

- What do you think my flaws are?
- What do I have a reputation for?
- Where do I require assistance?
- What obstacles do you foresee for me?

Now, I understand that this may make you feel really exposed at first. But believe me when I say that obtaining open and honest feedback is one of the most important initial actions you can take to better understand yourself and develop a solid foundation for your personal brand. One thing to keep in mind is that not all feedback is equal. Only pay attention to and act on comments from reliable sources. Avoid those who have a strong positive or negative bias. At the end of the day, knowing how people see you puts you in command of your personal brand and allows you to better shape it. Understand the importance of individuality: being distinctive does not necessitate dying your hair green. In truth, you don't need to make any changes to your look.

Consider each of your social media accounts as a landing page for your own brand. With that in mind, here are five things to think about when you go through your social media accounts. First and foremost, does your social media account correspond to your brand, company, and persona? Consider the searchability aspect. It will be much easier for others to locate you if you can get a handle that is your complete name. Even better, if possible, use the same handle for all channels and avoid using numerals or underscores.

Second, is your logo, company name, website, signature hashtag, and bio up to date and consistent across all platforms? If not, it's time to fine-tune each channel so that your brand is represented consistently across all channels. The third item, which is related to consistency, is to go through the information that has been released in the last several months. Do you publish on a consistent basis, or do you skip days, weeks, or even months without posting? The more consistent you are with your posting schedule, the more likely you are to grow your audience and increase interaction. Keep track of which content subjects and forms get the most attention and develop more of them. Give your audience what they want, and they'll return the favor by sharing it on their channels. As a result of this sharing and discussion of your content, search engines will be able to discover and distribute your products and services to more people.

Finally, and this is something I cannot emphasise enough, remember the 80/20 rule. On social media, this rule 80/20 refers to the proportion of non-promotional and promotional material. You should spend 80% of your time on social media, connecting with your community. You should spend 80% of your time on social media connecting with your community, participating in popular topics, and commenting on your followers' posts. You all know video is essential, but does the prospect of generating video content intimidate you, and do the words "live video" send chills up your spine? Let me bring you to a halt right there. There's no reason to be scared. When I meet with customers to talk about video, they frequently believe they'll need a cameraperson, editing abilities, or a large budget. Of course, this may appear intimidating, but the fact is that some of the finest methods to make and distribute video are through easy livestreaming programs that just require a smartphone, sufficient lighting, and sometimes a tripod. Now is the moment to take risks and take advantage of livestreaming.

Here are three easy methods to get started livestreaming right now. The first suggestion is to present some behind-the-scenes footage to your viewers. You all like to see what goes on behind the scenes, so show your audience how your company works. Maybe you're having a brainstorming session with your team, or you're putting up a booth at an expo, or you're going to deliver your first keynote address, and you're talking about how you're preparing. Don't overthink things, whatever you do. Instead, Allow the tale to unfold spontaneously. Instead of an overproduced infomercial, your audience wants a real and sympathetic inside view. It's critical to demonstrate the benefit of entering your world to your customers, and livestreaming allows you to do just that. The second method is to tease a new project and develop anticipation. Use that pop-up webcast to let the world know about a new project you're working on but haven't launched yet. You all like to feel like you're part of something exclusive, so your audience will appreciate having access to that information.

Here's a hint on how to do it. During the live video, ask your audience questions. This allows your audience to engage in what's going on, and it's enjoyable and exciting for them, because remember, when people like and comment on your feed, you'll receive more traffic and post shares. A call to action should always be included in live video material. Do you want them to subscribe to anything, follow you, or opt into a lead magnet, for example? Begin with the final aim in mind, and the story will fall into place. The third option is to demonstrate your product or, if you're an information-based personal brand, utilise the livestream to provide your audience with practical and relevant knowledge. So, when you know your audience will be watching, schedule your Facebook Live video and write a nice description for it. Inform them with the important details, such as where you are, what you're doing, and what they'll learn and why it will benefit them. You're all aware of the importance of samples to customers. Give them a sample that piques their interest makes them crave more. The way you promote ourselves changes as technology advances.

If you spend all of your time on your channels selling your brand and nothing else, people will quickly stop listening. Therefore, focus less on conversions and more on quality dialogues. As your audience grows, your audience insights will become increasingly important, which takes you to the fourth point. Do you utilise social media analytics software to track the growth, success, and involvement of your community? There's a reason why reality programs showcasing regular people doing ordinary things have fascinated us for so long.

Everything should be filtered via this question: would it help you achieve my desired reputation and legacy? Allow your brand to grow and change as it should. It's all about the journey rather than the destination. Don't leave it up to chance that others will perceive you in the manner you desire. Start today and take control of your personal brand by gaining influence and directing your reputation.

Remember to prioritise quality over quantity and ensure that you connect with your audience. Once you've gotten a decent handle on quality, increase the number of postings. Consider the following questions: Which aspects of my job do I excel at?

- What inspires you?
- What qualities have people commended you on?
- Which undertakings require the assistance of others on a regular basis?
- Which roles tend to sap my energy the most?
- Which tasks can I work on for several hours without becoming overwhelmed or exhausted?

You may choose how to effectively brand yourself after you're more aware of the many aspects of your personality. The ideal technique is to pick a certain area to concentrate on and let it grow over time. Your personal brand is more than a reflection of who you are now; it's a guide to where you want to go in the future. I recommend examining your strengths and weaknesses in relation to the sector or job you wish to break into next, in addition to knowing your current abilities and competencies. Employers will be curious as to why you're changing careers and how your talents and expertise transfer across sectors. Your personal brand, in addition to an effective resume and cover letter that showcase your transferable talents, aids you in telling your narrative to potential employers.

Although developing a personal brand may appear difficult, there are actions you can take to gain a reputation in your area. Here are five pointers to help you build a genuine personal brand while still advancing in your profession. You'll discover the abilities and attributes that distinguish you, as well as the areas where you need to develop or learn new information in order to progress. Forecasting where you want to be in five or ten years, as well as the qualities you want to be recognized for, can help you figure out what measures you need to take to get there. You must first decide on your target before you begin developing your own brand. Is it other thought leaders in the industry? a specific employee at a certain firm? Recruiters? The earlier you identify your audience, the easier it will be to construct your tale since you'll have a better idea of what kind of story you need to tell (and where you need to tell it.) Why? Because 92% of recruiters use social media to locate top prospects, with 87% of them using LinkedIn.

If you're a graphic designer looking to impress current clients and attract new ones, on the other hand, you might want to convey your narrative through a personal website or portfolio, where you can better display your many skills. I suggest accumulating research on specialists in such professions as you begin to sketch out the occupations you want. Find out who the thought leaders are in whatever sector you're interested in. and don't just follow them. Look them up on the internet to see whether they have blogs or other places where they share their ideas. Look for successful people and analyze what they're doing. Spend some time developing an elevator pitch—a 30- to 60-second tale about who you are—as you begin to define your personal brand.

LinkedIn is the ideal site for creating your identity and serving as a professional social media tool. Participating in groups, making introductions with individuals who interest you, and asking for (and giving) suggestions are the best ways to use this network. Other suggestions for expressing your story successfully on LinkedIn include: Concentrate on essential industry skills. Recruiters will frequently look for keywords related to the position they're attempting to fill, so be sure to include industry buzzwords in your profile—whether in your headline, summary, or job description—and explain your talents directly. Quantify your achievements. Simply stating that you're *"results-oriented"* isn't nearly as effective as demonstrating your successes.

When feasible, quantify your achievements, whether it's the number of articles you've published, the amount of money you've raised, or the number of transactions you've closed. Recruiters want to see your employment history, educational background, and a complete list of accomplishments, so be sure you're giving them all they need to know. Persuade them that you are the right person for the job. Use a professional photo: LinkedIn users who have a professional headshot get 14 times as many profile views as those who don't. Upload a recent photo of yourself that is tightly cropped to your face. Remember that you should be the center of attention, so stay away from crowded backdrops and smile. Recruiters are more likely to contact you if you appear friendly. Use this platform to promote and expand your industry knowledge. Use hashtags to focus on your specialisation, follow experts in your sector, and retweet top industry news to blend your own brand into your Twitter profile.

Remember that anything you tweet remains a part of your online persona. Aside from LinkedIn and Twitter, there are a slew of additional social media networks to explore. Choose the platforms where the people in your target audience and network spend their time. The following are some more social media networks to consider: While you might not think of Instagram as a career tool, it does provide users with a creative, visual platform on which to create their professional identity. Instagram is a particularly useful tool for people in the creative and digital marketing professions. Reddit is a prominent news and conversation network with over 52 million daily users. If you work in marketing or design, having a personal website or portfolio that offers critical information about who you are and aesthetically highlights your work is very important. This might mean you're seeking for a new job, have expertise in a certain field, or have just enhanced the worth of your present department or firm. It's critical to network consistently (and successfully) to expand your professional circle while you develop your ideal personal brand. Attend formal and casual networking events to meet colleagues and industry thought leaders.

Consider the last time you hired a genuine professional. A plumber, an electrician, a hairdresser, or even your dentist are all possibilities. How did you decide who you wanted to collaborate with? You probably used your network, asking friends, coworkers, and neighbors who they knew and loved. And there's a good probability you didn't thoroughly vet everyone. Rather than being based on a candidate's qualifications, skills, or experience, your decision was most likely influenced by someone you trust. And the problem is, that's not only how you employ your next roofer; it's also how you choose CEOs and board members, business partners, and team leaders.

These are the individuals you need to contact if you want to realise your aspirations and achieve your objectives. As a result, you can start forming significant connections in your network. Before you contact them, consider what they need to know about you and how you might help them. Also, keep in mind that these connections take time to develop. The stronger your bond, the more you'll be able to comprehend, support, and trust each other.

It's like a car salesperson selling you a car by explaining the parts of its engine when you simply talk about your talents. Sure, a tiny number of individuals will find it relevant, even fascinating, but the vast majority of people will be bored, confused, or both if presented with only that knowledge. When people ask you how much you're worth, instead of merely listing your abilities, connect them to projects and activities that you're skilled at but also like. This makes learning about your talents more engaging and relevant to your audience, as well as making it simpler for you to convey your strengths without coming off as boastful. Reading your CV is another major blunder you should avoid making during an interview or meeting. Now, I know you're not reading off your résumé, but introducing yourself by discussing your previous work experience, present job title, and position requirements is tedious.

Some people desire to stand out, yet they think bragging about oneself is arrogant and conceited. Whatever the reason, you might be squandering once-in-a-lifetime possibilities if you make blunders when attempting to explain your worth. In this session, I'll teach you how to avoid the most common blunders people make while attempting to speak about themselves in a professional context. The most common mistakes I've seen as a coach who routinely helps professionals prepare for interviews and company owners prepare for pitches are, first, conflating talents and value. Your particular strengths or characteristics are referred to as skills. They're the components that help you make an impression and contribute value. They're just not what people care about on their own.

One of the most significant things you can do to advance your career is to increase your social capital. It's not enough to be clear about your goals and understand which kinds of people fit into your pod as you build this high-impact social network. Another crucial component, if not the most crucial, is recognising how you may provide value to their lives. You'll be better equipped to define your worth and position yourself in a clear, compelling, and relevant manner after you've figured it out. Don't squander the limited time and attention you have by repeating the content on your LinkedIn page. Fascinate people instead. Share that genuinely engaging and important portion of your narrative if you want to attract their attention and their time. Keeping things absolutely professional is the final misstep committed during interviews and networking gatherings. I'm not suggesting you be unprofessional since you're talking about creating professional networks. I do recommend, though, that if you're asked to talk about yourself in order to find out what makes you unique, you disclose your entire self. Bring up a topic that you're enthusiastic about.

What distinguishes you from others?

Which is exactly what you're saying when you express your worth. So consider how you present yourself to the world. Who is aware of your existence? What information do they have about you? Is there someone in your life who needs a deeper knowledge of your worth? I encourage you to use all of the numerous channels available to you to express that value, whether it's at a team meeting, on your LinkedIn page, or in your resume.

Take a positive step forward today by expressing your worth. You can do it. You've chosen to stay a little longer so you can meet some new folks, but then you're going. So, what's the best approach to make the most of your time while still standing out and making an impression? I'll tell you what it isn't: presenting a scripted 30-second elevator pitch or talking about your work history. And yet, most of us do just that when someone asks, "What do you do?" or "Tell me about yourself." That is no longer the case. In this session, I'll reveal the shocking secret of how to create an impression and stand out in a crowd of dull people just by talking about what you care about.

Consider the last time you heard someone talk about something they were truly enthusiastic about. Before the big game, the coach's impassioned speech, a buddy talking about a new job she's genuinely thrilled to start, or a leader inspiring their team to a great finish What was your reaction to that? You grin more, your eyes open a little wider, you speak quicker, you lean in, and you feel better, happier, and more thrilled when you chat about topics that get you moving. Passionate brings energy, intensity, and emotion to the surface, and everyone on the receiving end feels it as well.

Practice expressing your passion in informal discussions during the following week. Talk to others about your interests. Keep an eye on how your attitude and facial expressions change and respond. You've just figured out how to make an impression. One of the simplest ways to leave a lasting impression and stand out in people's thoughts is to talk about topics you're passionate about and get them enthusiastic.

There's only one problem: it might be difficult to find an opportunity for passion issues in a professional setting. For example, typical interview and networking inquiries are predictable and frequently tedious. And you're stumped when asked, "What value do you contribute to your organisation?" Discuss your passion for travel or your domestic plant collection. In this class, I'll walk you through a simple method for passionately articulating your qualities and skills, demonstrating how amazing you are, and being recruited to do more of what you enjoy. Consider your working day.

There are certainly some projects and jobs that you like completing on a daily basis and others that you detest. What abilities do you bring to both kinds of initiatives that help you succeed? Would you rather be employed for the abilities you excel at and like, or for the ones you excel at but despise? It's self-evident that you'd like to have your schedule filled with chores that interest you. When you're asked to share a strength or showcase a talent, you typically default to talking about all of your strengths, regardless of whether or not you love putting them into practice.

How might you link them to resources in other sections of the company, or how might you enable someone from an underrepresented group who feels isolated and detached from the organisation to widen their network and boost their feeling of belonging? According to my study, people are four times more likely to speak the truth, behave properly toward others, and serve the organisation's larger good when they feel the organisation is fair and they have an equal chance of success. You enhance your reputation as a fair and honest person by ensuring that people you know have the same opportunities as everyone else. In doing so, you will have aided in the transformation of the rest of the organisation.

According to an old proverb, "The two most significant days in a person's life are the day they are born and the day they find out why." You're not alone if you've ever wished for greater significance in your life. I was fortunate to realise early in my career that my calling was to be a great change agent and to help others do the same. It's critical that others regard you as having a strong sense of purpose if you want to build a reputation for being trustworthy. I'm going to give you three ideas for finding a greater sense of purpose. You must first understand your own narrative. Knowing when you're at your best is essential. The first step in establishing a trustworthy reputation is knowing that you're spending your life for a cause that allows you to accomplish your best job and be the greatest version of yourself. Take the time to figure out what circumstances bring out the best in you, what ideals govern your decisions, and where and on whom you want to leave your imprint on the world. You and those you want to believe in you as a reliable person.

What do you consider to be your greatest achievements? When does your work provide you with the most pleasure? This is what I'd like you to do. Choose two or three scenes that you feel are record-breaking. Make a detailed outline of those stories. Go back and read them again to see if you can spot any trends. See what your tales tell, since understanding when you're at your best may help you figure out what offers you the most fulfillment. It's also crucial that you know what your values are. At your heart, you all have strongly held values that govern you.

Compassion, honesty, service, ambition, achieving results, and being productive are examples of values. People who adhere to a set of ideals are significantly more trustworthy than those who do not. Consider the previous four to five significant decisions you've made. Perhaps a significant purchase or a professional move. Pause the video and jot down your thoughts. Then, next to each decision, consider the underlying concepts that influenced your conclusion. What do you think you see? Do you have any values that serve you well? Knowing and adhering to a clearly defined set of values communicates to others that you are consistent and predictable in your responses to many situations. Finally, understanding your mission includes determining what larger benefit you wish to serve.

Unfortunately, this means you'll be employed to do jobs you both enjoy and despise. Stop promoting and displaying any strength. Instead, emphasize and discuss the abilities and strengths you use on tasks that you succeed at and like. This has two benefits: first, and I'll say it again, you'll get recruited and chosen to work on projects that you like and are good at. Another benefit is the enthusiasm with which you will be able to discuss your job, talents, and yourself in interviews and other meetings.

You're significantly more likely to become enthused and show your enthusiasm for what you do if you talk about chores, projects, occupations, and talents that you enjoy.

And one of the simplest ways to make other people interested in you and pay attention to you is to show them your enthusiasm. So, consider projects and occupations you've thoroughly enjoyed working on the next time you're trying to pick what abilities to highlight, whether for an interview or just interacting with other professionals. Determine two to three abilities that were utilized in those tasks. And as you explain your value, you'll begin to share it with the rest of the world.

Putting the puzzle pieces together. It's all about communicating who you are and why you matter when it comes to articulating your worth. There should be a takeaway, as with all stories. It should captivate your audience and leave them with an emotion, ideally excitement, or at the very least a desire to learn more about you. Unfortunately, most people make the mistake of presenting a thorough career biography or listing talents without connecting the links and expressing what influence they may have on their audience when talking about themselves in a professional setting. Have you ever done something like that? How might you link them to resources in other sections of the organisation, such as someone who works in a support role and doesn't have access to the resources they need to make the improvements they want?

You'll be able to tell the difference between sharing your abilities and sharing your effects following this course. You'll have a system in place that allows you to rapidly make the connections between what you're good at and why it matters. You'll also be able to express your effects to others clearly. What are some of your best qualities? Consider the three or so tasks in which you excel and that you genuinely like. Perhaps you're a natural problem solver or excel at data analysis. Many of the professionals I know have good interpersonal skills and use them to help and raise others.

Your abilities are valuable, but they are meaningless if you are unable to link them to a positive influence. It's nice to hear you're a wordsmithing magician, but I'm more interested in what you can achieve with that skill. The difference between a skill and an impact is this. A talent is a technical edge or ability that you have. What you can do with your expertise determines your effect. It's all about how you transfer your strength into a useful deed or result for others. So, first, make a list of at least three abilities you'd like to share with the rest of the world.

When it came time to put the strategy into action, her people skills came in handy since she was able to identify and collaborate with the necessary personnel to achieve a more optimised onboarding process. So give it a shot by charting the relationship between your skills and their influence. Take a piece of paper or, better yet, record yourself speaking. Now you must respond to this question. How are you now using, or have you previously utilised, a highly talented person to accomplish anything notable?

Humans are innately selfish, or perhaps egotistical is a better term. Your entire universe revolves around you. You, on the other hand, are mainly concerned with yourself. It may not be pleasant to hear, but it is true. And it isn't always a negative thing, but I'll explain why in a moment. The reason I'm bringing this up now is so you understand that demonstrating your abilities to others isn't enough. Connecting the links and demonstrating your influence isn't enough. People want to know how your abilities and effects will directly help them.

They must comprehend without a shadow of a doubt that you can either solve an issue for them or make a major difference in their life. When you witness someone suffering from a migraine, you may empathise with their suffering because you egocentrically compare it to your own migraines. That may persuade you to talk more slowly or offer them pain medication.

Since its inception in 2010, Instagram has come a long way. The 'Gram, which started out as a simple photo-sharing app, has evolved into a variety of things, including a way to reconnect with old friends, a place to start new flings, a portfolio for creatives of all kinds to showcase their work, a battleground for social justice, a shopping and e-commerce platform, and a gallery of whatever NFTs are. Finally, Instagram has become a reflection of your values, which the all-seeing Algorithm reminds us of every time you check in. The software has even aided in the emergence of a new type of celebrity. Instagram influencers have altered how you scroll, how you are amused, and even how marketers sell their products to you. When it comes to the greatest stars on Instagram, though, you notice some familiar faces. Cristiano Ronaldo, for example, recently became the first human to reach 400 million follors on Instagram, with Kylie Jenner not far behind. In addition, Instagram's own profile surpassed half a billion followers, music artists continued to trade places, and a new Kardashian joined the top 10.

National Geographic, with 169 million followers, and Nike, with 159 million followers, are two well-known businesses that have acquired large Instagram followings on their own. Most brands, on the other hand, are way past their capacities. Working with one or more influencers allows an ordinary firm to reach a considerably larger audience.

Finding social media influencers may be difficult for companies. That is why influencer platforms were created in the first place: to make the process of finding influencers for businesses easier. It's not easy to figure out who the top Instagram influencers are, and it'd be tough to say who the top 25 Instagram influencers are unequivocally. The niche in which a person works has a big impact on their influence. You can't judge someone by their number of followers; the most popular Instagram accounts tend to belong to celebrities, and whatever impact they have is due to their celebrity status rather than their Instagram prowess. Many non-mainstream areas have Instagram accounts run by people who are acknowledged as experts in their field but have lower followings. Because of the limited support for that genre, many non-mainstream genres have people operating Instagram profiles that are acknowledged as experts in their industry but have fewer follower numbers. In fact, even within a specialty, depending on follower numbers isn't a fair indicator of impact. In actuality, to be an influencer, you must engage your audience rather than merely broadcast.

When people make a good effect on others, they experience their greatest feeling of fulfillment. Serving a larger cause beyond your personal interests allows you to combine your greatest moments and the ideals that govern your life into an indelible imprint on the world that only you can leave. What is the long-term worth of your work to others? Do you get a great feeling of satisfaction from knowing this? What would need to be altered in your career or life to make that connection a reality if you struggle to see a direct link between your abilities, values, and effects on others?

Consider a period when someone offered you the chance to flourish and grow. Do you recall how you felt at the time? Looking for methods to help others shine and feel the same way about you is one of the most critical things you can do to establish a trustworthy reputation. Here are five easy ways to get started. To begin with, provide opportunities for others to showcase their abilities by having them give presentations at critical meetings. Whether you're hosting or attending a meeting, you may persuade the host to include time on the schedule for someone to share an idea, make progress on a project they're working on, or pitch a project they believe in.

Second, if you're working on a high-profile project, invite someone to join you to expose them to a wider audience inside the organisation. Perhaps they will contribute special skills that the project requires, or it will be an opportunity for them to develop their network. Working on projects with a lot of visibility allows others to see their greatest work. Finally, you could know anything about someone's professional goals or individuals in their network that they'd want to meet. Introduce them to individuals who might help them progress their careers, serve as a mentor, and keep them on your radar for future possibilities where they could be a good fit.

Consider now and later when it comes to the legacy you wish to leave. What are you doing today, strategically, that will have an influence on the legacy you leave later? This is an extremely essential topic to consider, but one that you sadly cannot always manage. However, reconsider your strategy. So, what do you want to achieve in the end? Do you wish to help the environment as a philanthropist? So, concentrate on it. Make sure you don't become sidetracked by other areas since, as you previously stated, there is a lot of good work to be done in the world, and it's tempting to attempt to accomplish a number of various things, especially if you have a variety of abilities that take you down other paths.When it comes to your legacy, though, you'll be recognised for the work you accomplished. So, what are you doing right now to sow seeds that will bear fruit in the future? When you're no longer here, what will people say about you? What did you do that had a lasting impact? And the best way to do so is to think strategically about what's going on right now and how it will affect how you're remembered afterwards.

Positive self-talk is important. When you believe in ourselves, our thoughts and bodies work in tandem to help us achieve our goals. Your body will do what you tell it to do, which is why sending positive signals to ourselves is so vital. It matters what you believe. Because everything you do is psychosomatic, it matters what you think. As a result, what you represent to others is how you feel about yourself. First and foremost, don't allow anybody else to define you. Your personal tale is written by you. You are the only one who can determine who you are and what your abilities and talents are. They're one-of-a-kind. You seek out such possibilities and methods to put them to good use in ways that benefit you as ll as society. As a result, if you don't believe in yourself, others may not either. Because your ideas, whether you believe it or not, will work for or against you. Because everyone is different, it's more vital to recognize that.

The outcomes are genuine if you understand and accept yourself. And there's a lovely sincerity to the way you go about your lives and jobs. Other people can detect when you're being genuine since you're wired to recognize the difference between a fake and a genuine person. So whether you're being real or not, there's something off, and people can sense it if you're not, and that will set the tone for how you engage with them. You may notice that when someone isn't being honest, you can't quite put your finger on it, but you know something isn't right, and it's something you want to avoid in your personal and professional lives. Life is too short.

Because everyone is different, it's extremely crucial to remember who you are. You want to be your authentic self so that you may project it to others and help the world improve. And, because what you believe counts, when you truly express yourself, others will accept you. And that is how the world gets changed for the better.

Many of us find it difficult to comprehend what authenticity entails in the abstract. When it's concrete, you can wrap our arms around it much more easily. This is why it's crucial to tell your story. Finally, by sharing your story, you may demonstrate authenticity. Some firms have adopted a variant of this technique when employees speak to an internal or external audience. Sharing personal tales has the advantage of modeling real platforms that are appropriate for the company. There are three basic stages to telling your tale. First, come up with a personal tale that reflects the organisation's inclusive principles. I'm not talking about professional achievements here; rather, I'm talking about personal tales that reveal who you are.

I'm not talking about professional achievements here; rather, I'm talking about personal tales that go beyond the scope of a standard résumé. After that, make any required changes for a professional setting. This simply entails ensuring that the narrative is acceptable in a professional context, and then considering sharing it with an internal or external audience when introducing oneself.

The typical adult's attention span nowadays is between seven and twelve seconds, putting pressure on us to captivate and grab your viewers right away. So, how do you go about doing that? Consider the last time you attended a conference or listened to a great podcast or webinar. I'm sure you remember the tales and experiences that were given, but you probably don't recall any of the data or figures that were provided. Your brains are wired to recall tales, not numbers, and the power of storytelling is contagious. As a result, you should include it in your brand assets and content marketing activities.

Now, keep in mind that the goal of your personal brand narrative isn't to promote yourself excessively. The idea is to connect your experience to the audience's problems and show how you can help them. You become more remembered and trusted when your audience can relate to and learn from you as a genuine person. And your audience will be more eager to learn more about you and collaborate with you.

Who are your current clients, and why did they choose to do business with you? See where the common thread is by looking for shared pain areas, features, and hobbies. Have you discovered any trends or key words as a result of working with these clients that you can use to improve your service descriptions or marketing messaging? It's extremely probable that your product or service will help others who are similar to them. The second suggestion is to know all there is to know about your product or service. Choose precise demographics to target since greater clarity leads to more conversions. Age, location, gender, income, education level, marriage or family status, and employment are all things to consider. Take into account the psychographics, or the more personal attributes, of an ideal candidate.

Personality, values, motivators, interests, hobbies, and way of life are just a few examples. The fourth and last tip is to figure out where your target demographic hangs out on social media. It's quite possible that a new consumer will find you on social media in today's technologically and socially linked society. As a result, you want to know which social media platform draws your target audience. Then be sure to post material and stay active on the platform. Be where your target market is. Check out the social media demographics exercise file for additional information on social media demographics and how to figure out which channels you should be most active on. You'll be glad you did it.

Your personal brand is also affected by the why of branding and the how of marketing. Prior to and throughout any marketing initiatives, branding is crucial. This procedure is commonly misunderstood and the target of considerable scorn when it comes to personal branding. Many people make the mistake of beginning with personal branding, which entails understanding and connecting, rather than personal marketing, which involves developing and communicating.

Personal branding isn't just for people who are active in the public eye. You can demonstrate your abilities regardless of who you are.

CHAPTER THREE

Building Brand Through Social Media Marketing

"Your brand is your public identity, what you're trusted for. And for your brand to endure, it has to be tested, redefined, managed, and expanded as markets evolve. Brands either learn or disappear."

The term "social media marketing" describes commercial activity on social media platforms that supports marketing goals including brand exposure, website traffic, and client acquisition. The majority of this activity takes the form of content, such as writing, photographs, and videos, but it also involves sponsored advertisements and community involvement. The audience's desire to spread the material is at the core of excellent social media content. Your audience becomes your distribution channel when they spread your material.

Content that is extremely relevant and aesthetically pleasing is likely to generate significant interaction and sharing, whether someone tags a buddy in an Instagram image or tweets it to their audience. For specific corporate goals, some social media platforms perform better than others, and the published material will change based on these variables. For instance, it's doubtful that a Facebook video would drive more business audience visits than a LinkedIn post, and so on. The wonderful thing about this is that you can use the functions of various social media platforms for various marketing campaigns, making sure the material is exceptionally suited for that platform and audience. More on this in the strategies section!

How to make your social networking platform the most successful? There is no simple solution to this, and social media marketing is not a cure-all approach. What advantages can social media marketing strategies offer? As previously said, the particular business results of social media marketing efforts (such as sales, traffic, etc.) will depend on the initial objectives you establish. However, there are more general advantages to companies using social media, such as:

- Being easier to find.
- You're more likely to be found by new potential clients if you post material on a variety of social media platforms that is customised to your target market.
- Having fruitful discussions with customers.
- It makes sense that so many businesses host Q&As on Instagram Stories or use Twitter for customer service. A friendly and casual technique to get to know your audience is through social media marketing.
- More than ever, social media marketing makes it simple to introduce the world to a company's culture and its

employees. This helps when attracting outstanding new employees and also boosts client loyalty!

- Establishing a community.
- Regardless of your sector, social media marketing may help you establish connections with your target market and other pertinent companies.
- With every new app release, more original strategies to improve your social media marketing and achieve those KPIs are introduced.

The advantages are limitless, and you'll profit more from social media marketing as you gain knowledge of the platforms and content that suit your goals the best.

"Think about what people are doing on Facebook today. They're keeping up with their friends and family, but they're also building an image and identity for themselves, which in a sense is their brand. They're connecting with the audience that they want to connect to. It's almost a disadvantage if you're not on it now." -Mark Zuckerberg

How to establish your core brand values?

Right now, social media marketing is enormous, and for good reason. Businesses may use these channels to bring their brand online and create awareness. Those same businesses may also engage their clients online and respond to customer care concerns rapidly. Paid advertising has a wide range of alternatives as well. Companies can use targeted alternatives to find the folks they're looking for. The possibilities are nearly endless, which means that firms may make use of these platforms in a variety of ways.

"A brand is the set of expectations, memories, stories and relationships that, taken together, account for a consumer's decision to choose one product or service over another."– Seth Godin

When someone is analysing your professional abilities, they will frequently resort to LinkedIn to discover more about you. The good news is that they'll succeed even if they don't start at LinkedIn and instead start at Google. Because your LinkedIn profile will almost certainly appear at the top of the search results. You know that the top three links get 62% of all clicks. As a result, individuals will find their way to your LinkedIn profile. That's where you should concentrate your efforts. Now, your LinkedIn profile isn't the instrument you use to look for work. LinkedIn is now the location where you can improve your work performance and brag about how fantastic you are to the rest of the world. You'll concentrate on three crucial elements: your headshot, headline, and summary. Let's start with your profile picture. The internet is a strange, hazy realm. People want to be able to associate a face with some material in order for us to be credible. So you'll want to concentrate on getting a high-quality professional headshot—no selfies, no photographs of you chopped out of a picture with your arm around someone else.

How do you think I'll feel if I hire you, or if I hire you, or if I promote you? Your reputation is your own brand. It's your legacy, after all. It explains what others may anticipate from you. Personal branding is a simple procedure, but it is not easy. I'm going to urge you to consider topics that could push you beyond your comfort zone in this course. However, as a result, you will have a competitive edge. You'll understand how to position yourself in relation to others. It's all about control when it comes to personal branding. Do you enjoy having the upper hand? Control is what I adore. To me, control entails making a decision. It denotes a range of possibilities.

Building influence with your workplace's decision makers and collaborators requires not just the ability to recognize and respond to their demands but also the development of a plan for how you want to be recognized. Now, I'd want to take this opportunity to discuss credibility, since without it, no personal brand is worth anything. So, let's speak about the formula for establishing your own brand's reputation. There is no way around it. Values plus action equals credibility, which is the formula for establishing credibility. To begin with, you must be very clear about your values. What are your core values? What is so fundamental to your moral fiber and DNA that you wouldn't be you if it wasn't present? What are your core values?

Many of you are performing excellent jobs, making excellent judgments, and living a life of integrity, but you aren't telling others why. You're not giving credit for that activity because you're not tying it to the value. And you do need credibility to establish influence in the areas of personal branding and job growth. So, I'd like you to think about your beliefs right now. Consider what you truly believe in and be as detailed as possible. Keep your distance from the fluff. Drill deep into your values and ask yourself how you're putting them into practice. Remember how I said personal branding was all about having control? So, here's how you're going to reclaim your power. I'd want you to join me for a few minutes at a place that might be a bit unsettling. I'd like you to pretend that you're at your memorial service. Your friends and family are on the other side of the room, and they knew you well. They knew all there was to know about you, including your whole life narrative. But I'd like you to consider those of us on the other side, those of us who worked with you, served with you, or were part of a community with you.

This first point came about as a result of the internet's immense power. You may reconnect with long-lost acquaintances, meet new people, and do it all from the comfort of your own home using a platform like social media. It's amazing how interconnected you've all become as a result of these platforms. It's a tremendous thing to be able to communicate with anyone, anywhere on the planet.

Capture words, feelings, and sentiments so you can start developing a strategy to advance your career. Would you spend money advertising in adolescent publications, high schools, or regions where people don't drive automobiles if you were a premium car brand like Mercedes-Benz? Probably not. Probably because kids can't afford your automobile, even if they wish they could, and non-drivers aren't interested in car firms. You'll promote your goods to those who find the offer of your brand's experience exciting and appealing, as well as those who can afford it.

Personal branding, on the other hand, functions in the same manner. You market and position yourself to certain audiences who will find you interesting and relevant. This is when things become a bit complicated. You must determine who your target audience is. Who are the individuals, communities, businesses, and even sectors who need to find you? Start by considering the people with whom you have the most success. Who do you have a connection with? When you're working with someone, do you feel like you're on the same page? If you're looking for a job or changing employment, your target audience will likely include people from other firms or beyond your direct circle of influence.

You're going to use the internet to establish your brand. At least in a professional capacity, you need just one tool to establish your online identity, and that tool is LinkedIn, and here's why. You want it to be as professional as possible. You also want your face to take up the majority of the frame because it typically seems quite tiny. So you want people to be able to emotionally connect with you.

Once you've done this, you'll have the means to interact and engage with people. Once you've done this, they'll want to learn more about you.It encourages individuals to read more. That means there will be no dull headlines. If you don't specify a headline, LinkedIn will use your current job title as your headline. And, to be honest, that's a snooze. So, how do you go about doing it? The first section is your job title or key terms with which you wish to be linked. It's critical because it assists you in being found and relevant. The second factor is your business.

You want to demonstrate your tight ties and commitment to the firm where you work. You don't have to grasp every social media site to be technologically brilliant and appealing. LinkedIn goes a long way for busy, clever professionals like you. Simply visit your profile on a regular basis, change your picture, headline, and summary, and remain active on LinkedIn. Your goal for you is to learn and connect on LinkedIn for roughly nine minutes every week.

You set yourself up for a whole professional explosion when you grow your brand online and make it as engaging as your real-world brand. It's possible that you're what, or that your sole area of skill is creating headlines for print advertising. It might be as simple as using the most recent behavioral psychology research to create headlines that convert readers into purchasers. These three requirements must also be met by your unique field of expertise. Passion. The subject energises you; simply thinking about it makes you eager. aspiration It is relevant to your job and will assist you in reaching your goals. Also, dedication. You're committed to doing whatever it takes to stay current in your field. Also, keep in mind that your area of knowledge may not be limited to your job function. It might be anything marketing-related, or it could be your opinions on connection development or teamwork if you work in marketing.

You go to Starbucks because they satisfy your emotional requirements and you're a committed customer of their brand and goods. When you go through the door, you get a sense of belonging, and it's a little kitschy. People recognize their drink, and you know how to order it, and you appreciate their product. So you're not just receiving a cup of coffee, but you're also getting a sense of belonging to a community and culture that you value. It's critical to understand what your target audience expects from you while you're thinking about them. Perhaps they want you to be on time and on budget, as well as possess certain technical abilities, but what do they expect from you?

You must determine how that individual, community, or sector should feel. It's usually not that difficult. Many individuals desire to feel secure. They want to be able to put their faith in you. They want to experience a sense of kinship or participation with you. But pay attention to what keywords or indications you have of what your target audience needs to experience, whether you're talking to them, connecting with them, or studying them online. Then you'll consider, "How can I make myself appealing to that target audience?"

In terms of personal branding, authenticity entails being aware of how you present yourself. It involves being aware of the initial impression you'll create, which can frequently determine how others see you, and it starts with your style and appearance. It all starts with the realization that your personal brand requires you to look like yourself, not someone else. Dress comfortably but also appropriately for the audience and occasion. So, if you're speaking to a huge group of financial executives at a business event, you're not going to wear a baseball cap and tattered jeans and shoes; instead, you'll dress appropriately for the occasion, but in a way that makes you feel confident.

So, today, I'd like to share few distinct body language ideas with you. The first step is to make eye contact. Look someone in the eyes when you're chatting to them. Make good eye contact with them to show that you respect them and that you are paying attention to them. Don't make eye contact for too long or it will become awkward or unpleasant. This is because eye contact may occasionally veer into intimacy or even threatening territory. As a result, maintain acceptable eye contact. When you need to break eye contact, simply turn away for a few moments or glance at something else to convey some comfort. So, if you're speaking to a huge group of financial executives in a business forum, you're not going to dress in a baseball cap and tattered jeans and shoes; instead, you're going to dress in a way that makes you feel like yourself and promotes your values and personal brand. If you stay honest and connect your actions with those tactics, you'll be able to match your body language and image to the person you are on the inside and the person you want others to see.

You must know who you are and what you stand for.

How can you present yourself in the best possible light and in the best possible circumstances to begin that relationship? What emotional connection can you establish with your viewers or clients in order to establish a friendship and exert influence? Are there any possibilities? Maybe you passed up possibilities because you didn't feel secure or ready to lean in, but now that you know what you want your reputation to look like, you want to seize those opportunities. Your plan must have a beginning and an end point, as well as metrics to monitor progress and make course changes if necessary.

"The keys to brand success are self-definition, transparency, authenticity and accountability." – Simon Mainwaring

You want to be considered for a partner position at your company, or you want to be a part of more critical management discussions. So, what will it take for people to regard you as trustworthy and relatable and someone they should bring up in such discussions? Perhaps you should speak out more at meetings. Raise your hand if you want to share your thoughts. Perhaps you should contribute to the corporate blog and lend your voice to the discussion. Perhaps you might network internally more strategically so that you can get clout with individuals who are inviting people to those gatherings. Then you know you're on the correct track when those things start to happen and you see the outcomes in the metrics. And if it doesn't work, you'll pivot and try something different, always keeping your desired reputation in mind. It's all about taking small steps toward establishing your brand.

Allow others to see what you are passionate about and what you are interested in. Also, keep in mind that everything you do online is public; it all serves to demonstrate what you stand for, what you're passionate about, and what you're interested in to others. So, if you're commenting on things or sharing photographs that you believe would go unnoticed or that a hiring manager might overlook, don't do it. Also, keep your eyes peeled for your target audience on the internet. Where are they? If you want to attract the attention of business executives and professionals, you'll undoubtedly spend a lot of time on LinkedIn, because that's where they hang out.

"Brand is the sum total of how someone perceives a particular organization. Branding is about shaping that perception." -Ashley Friedlein

Traditional businesspeople that have built a strong personal brand leverage that influence to expand their credibility network and, of course, money. Smart business owners are not only investing in their own personal brand development and growth, but they are also pushing their staff to do the same. Consider this: your staff are in the best position to talk about and share your product, and consumers are more inclined to believe their recommendations than those of a large organisation. It's all about getting acceptance from your peers. If you don't believe me, consider this: brand messages disseminated by workers are reshared twenty-four times more frequently than brand messages, and leads generated by employee social marketing convert seven times more frequently than other leads. Personal brands are undeniably strong, but the point I'm trying to make here is that they can be utilised in conjunction with your corporate brand to achieve even greater outcomes. Building your own brand can be quite rewarding, both personally and professionally, as you'll discover.

Because authenticity is so important in personal branding, you'll want to show off your actual personality to your audience and consumers. You can't do that until you're being real, and you can't be authentic unless you're shining a light. And you won't be able to achieve it unless you understand yourself. What have you contributed in life? How much of it was done on purpose? What are your remaining goals and why are they important to you? What are your special abilities or superpowers? Okay, the next question is a biggie. What gives you authority? "Brand yourself before others do," as the phrase goes. So, think about it: what talents have you learned throughout the course of your life? What qualifications, credentials, certificates, accolades, or proven success stories do you have to back up your claims? If you want to be renowned for anything, you need to be actively writing about it, participating in popular debates, and attending conferences or summits on the subject.

It's critical to define your target market. You can't satisfy everyone when it comes to selling your services. Consider who will gain the most from your products or services. Is it single mothers, college students, first-time home purchasers, job hunters, or telecommuters? Consumer demographics may not be at the top of your mind, but trust me when I say that the more defined your target group is, the faster you'll expand your network and convert more consumers. A target audience is a set of people who are more likely to need and purchase what you're selling. Here are ways and means to help you locate your target audience.

Be honest with yourself about your area of expertise and how you can help your clients. This will highlight what your offer should include in particular. Here are some important questions to consider: "How can you bundle your knowledge into a product or service?"

- Is it one-on-one coaching, a group workshop in person, an online webinar, or an ebook, for example?
- What channel, approach, or platform is ideal for showcasing your knowledge and assisting clients in seeing results?
- What is the demand for your service, and who has those requirements?
- What outcomes will your service or product provide, and who will benefit the most?
- What is the price of your service or product, and how much does it cost?
- How much does your service or product cost, and is this individual able to pay it?
- What are some possible complaints about the service, product, offering, and price?
- Who are your rivals, and who is their target audience?

The answers to all of these questions will assist you in creating a clear and complete profile of your ideal consumer. The next piece of advice is to construct your buyer's character now that you have a better knowledge of your product.

There is no substitute for preparedness. You may get into character and bake till your heart's content, but if you're not prepared, it will show. By neglecting to prepare, you're planning to fail, as Benjamin Franklin put it. And I can absolutely attest to that. As a result, I strongly advise you to be prepared. Preparation also entails paying attention to the subject at hand. It's ensuring that you're saying, "I'm concerned enough about this to attempt to be prepared." It boosts your confidence since you know you've got this. And if you're prepared on a fundamental level, you have the flexibility to be virtually artistic with whatever you're doing. It gives you the opportunity to grow. It gives you the ability to express yourself creatively. It gives you the flexibility to add to things. Because you're completely prepared, it gives you the ability to pivot a little bit more.

The healthy sense of humility, one that will allow you to continue to develop, because you all realize you are flawed. You appreciate all of the good aspects of yourselves in the same way that you did in tool number one. You take everything in and then let it go, learning from it. However, the best example I can offer you is that all professional and successful people have mentors. Everyone should have a mentor because you need that objective viewpoint to help you progress. If you believe you are constantly on top of your game, you may find yourself falling behind. So it's crucial to remember to surround yourself with people and communities. So, remember to surround yourself with people you can trust and who can provide you with objective perspectives as well as those with whom you can share your own. And also to get encouragement from it, because it's crucial to realize that there's always an opportunity for improvement.

Be fully conscious of who you are and completely accepting of who you are. This boosts one's self-esteem. When you know who you are and are completely comfortable with it, it makes it easier for others to do the same. It also assists you in living and working in a real manner. Isn't it true that life is an evolutionary process?

You get through it and go about your daily lives. Every day brings us new experiences. And, whether you realize it or not, each of those events shapes how you conduct your lives. You are affected by them. As a result, you must keep track of what is occurring to you on a daily basis. There's a lovely way of taking things in and not keeping them. Do not cling to them. You welcome them in, acknowledge their presence, and then let them depart. And you take what you can from them. So there's a bad and a positive side to this. Whatever it is, you take it in. You don't hang on to it because if it's negative, it will almost surely affect you negatively. However, there may be something to be learned from this. If it's positive, you don't want to cling to it too tightly because you want to maintain your humility. Whatever it is, know yourself, accept yourself, and live each day. Glean from each day, and learn from each day. Accept them, allow them to strengthen you, and then let them go.

"Branding demands commitment; commitment to continual re-invention; striking chords with people to stir their emotions; and commitment to imagination. It is easy to be cynical about such things, much harder to be successful."- Jeff Bezos

You must clarify your point of view in order to become the go-to expert or thought leader. What is your strong point of view in your field of competence? For example, if you work in print advertising, you may assume that producing innovative, zany, and completely unexpected material is the key to success. Or maybe you're the type of writer who thinks every headline should be backed up by psychological research and properly vetted. So it's a matter of taking your knowledge and adding your viewpoint to it. To give you an example, you're both professionals at assisting high achievers.

Make an effort to empathize. Use it to gain a deeper understanding of your audience's problems. Then explain how you can help them by providing a solution to their problem. Your value proposition is the precise advantage you deliver. It's the key to their hearts, and it's what your audience finds most intriguing and compelling. To create a compelling value offer, you must first understand the genuine problems that someone is attempting to solve. Active listening can help you obtain this vital information. Pay attention when others express their wants and disappointments. What is the true answer you are offering, and how are you fundamentally improving their lives? Nothing suffocates confidence like the belief that you must be flawless in order to be respected. Giving up the act and figuring out what made you good enough, if not exceptional, made a huge impact in your professional life. I'll tell you how to let go of unrealistic expectations and discover comfort and true success in simply being yourself. There's nothing wrong with wanting to learn more and experience more. Striving for perfection may be energising. Expecting oneself to be flawless, on the other hand, is a recipe for disaster. Perfection is impossible to achieve. Strive for it, and you'll never feel good enough, which will make you concerned about your performance, causing you to show up looking and feeling uneasy.

You don't have to be flawless to be outstanding at anything. The majority of your worth comes from learning how to successfully harness your skills and talents to satisfy the needs of your team, company, and clients. To put it another way, you're more than your degrees, knowledge, or technical talents. Being kind, for example, may not appear to be an important professional ability until you realise that being pleasant means you show up in problem-solving situations as fair, helpful, and collaborative. Now it's your turn.

Rather than attempting to be flawless, embrace your own unique self. To fulfill the demands of your present work environment, identify, reinterpret, and exploit your existing abilities. It's always best to show up as you are. Have the mindset of a distinctive brand. It's about aligning all of your contact points behind a single mindset. Consider that for a moment. There are numerous companies that you admire and trust, and you may purchase their items. This holds true in the field of personal branding as well. Michael Jordan is a fantastic example. His entire ideology, and everything he would be associated with, was based on winning, winning, winning. This was evident in his own philosophy. The good news is as follows: You, too, can build a successful personal brand. All you have to do now is figure out your own personal why. It's all about winning for Michael Jordan. All you need is a clear objective for yourself. In a year's time, where do you picture yourself? When you have a goal in mind, you may direct your energies toward it. And that, my friends, is how you can create something that will help you succeed and stand out from the crowd. I'd want you to do the following. Make a one-year goal for yourself. This is a very particular professional objective. Let me give you a few instances. You might desire to increase your earnings. With your existing employment, you might desire to take on greater responsibility. You could wish to further your career, whether at your present employer or elsewhere, or you might want to start your own business.

How to modestly promote oneself—Who will stand out for you if you don't?

Job opportunities come and go. Job security is a thing of the past. Number one, you know that many experts consider self-promotion to be a filthy term, which only you can spot. It's funny, though, that it's the successful professionals, the ones who are always up for promotion, who understand that keeping quiet about their accomplishments would lead to their being undervalued and disregarded. They understand that in order to be remembered and acknowledged, they must also brag about themselves. I am going to show you how to self-promote comfortably, genuinely, and even humbly. The first step is to adjust your mentality. Self-promotion must be reframed as sharing and service. When people are aware of the various ways you may add value, they will want to learn more about you and have access to what you have to offer. Take note of how, in most circumstances, good enough is, well, good enough.

Not every task will necessitate your finest degree of performance. So, depending on the assignment, you'll want to aim for a standard that's somewhere between good enough and great. If you have more time, try establishing weekly objectives to help you attain your monthly goal. Keep in mind that you may still make changes to this along the way if you achieve a target faster in one week than in the next; it's all okay. There are countless choices as long as you are taking measures to become a success story in your mind to attain your one-year target. Visualising success is just planning, and when you have a plan and picture success, you'll discover ways to stand out and be ready when the chance to achieve what you consider success and expand your business occurs.

Humans are sociable creatures. The people you trust in your lives, the individuals in your circle, are supported, elevated, and promoted by others. Both sides can benefit from the trust you develop in your relationships by seizing critical chances. This is where social capital comes in. The potential prospects arising from all of your network's relationships are referred to as social capital. The universe revolves around social capital. Working hard or being the most competent, educated, or senior person in the room isn't enough at the end of the day. If you want to advance professionally, you need to tap into the social capital of your network to gain access to the most lucrative possibilities. That's why it's critical for you to clearly state what you do and why you're doing it. You can't wait until you're in desperate need of a network to start putting one together.

Building your network and increasing your social capital should be strategic. Aim to build a network that recognises your worth, trusts you, and knows you well enough to help you achieve your goals by sharing your worth with the right people at the appropriate time. Create a method to keep track of who you're reaching out to on a frequent and meaningful basis as you reach out. To get started, create a list of people who are already in your professional social network. These are the folks with whom you're already in contact at work, in your professional places, and in your greater professional sphere. Make a second list of individuals you'd like to add to your network after that.

You had no influence when you were born. You are born on this planet without any preconceived notions. Your parents are your first and arguably most powerful influence. Innocent phrases meant to protect you, such as "be cautious when jumping from bed," if repeated often enough, can stifle your willingness to take chances, might deter you from following your aspirations. After that, you'll look at the educational system. One that forces us to choose only one item to commit to. You may be urged to choose societally dependable courses like science or math in order to increase your chances of success. Alternatively, you may be influenced by the professional choices of your peers.

Connecting with others who can benefit from what you have to give is the objective of social media. Creating the perfect client profile is one way to do this. Boost your chances of striking up a meaningful conversation by knowing who you're talking to. The first thing you should do is consider current projects you've worked on and individuals with whom you enjoy interacting. You're on the lookout for someone who could be interested in purchasing your goods or services in the future. You must generate material that is appealing to your target customer if you want to engage with them. Exploring other sites and profiles in your field is one method to achieve this. That way, you'll have a better idea of what's out there and what kind of material people are responding to. Taking advantage of social media as a tool What did you do after setting a goal last year to become a personal brand leader in communications? Every week, you'd go on LinkedIn Live, and you continue to do it today to broadcast video interviews with successful individuals in the fields of communications, health, and entrepreneurship. You'd also give advice on how others might achieve success by using communication and awareness. Every week, you've been consistent. Why? because every time you wrote a blog article on these two topics, it was indexed by LinkedIn's search engines.

People with a good reputation are recognised for partnering with others and assisting them in achieving the goals they've aspired to but haven't been able to achieve. Let's talk about what you can do to ensure that everyone in your network and sphere of influence has an equal opportunity at success. Here are three actions you may take to help. To begin with, be open and honest about any prejudices you or your company may have against particular categories of people. It might be that specific components of identification, such as skin color, race, gender, or ethnicity, are underrepresented and undervalued in your company, or that certain positions are undervalued. Those in support roles, those without specific qualifications, or those whose occupations aren't critical to the organisation's goal. Identify four or five people in your network who you feel are being harmed by prejudices that are preventing them from achieving their goals. Second, think about areas where you or others in your network may or may not have earned credentials. Perhaps you belong to a demographic group that is well-represented in your company, or you work in a position that provides you with unique benefits since it is so important to the organisation's goal.

Speak with emotion. Share areas of your personality that aren't related to work. If familiarity and trust are important factors in establishing social capital, you want people to feel like they know you well enough. It's now your turn. Consider the last three people you encountered in a professional setting. Is there anyone who stands out among them? What made them interesting or uninteresting? What are some things you wish people knew about you? It's not just for networking or interviewing that you should be articulating your worth. Getting adept at talking about yourself, also known as value articulation, is a talent that may help you in more ways than just getting hired or promoted. You'll be able to spot chances to express your worth throughout your workday and beyond after watching this session. I want you to start expressing value with confidence and clarity, which will help you advance in your work and in your daily life.

Today, it's incredibly simple for someone to set up a website and claim to be an expert. The worst thing you can do is declare yourself a thought leader without having the necessary experience or education. So start thinking about where you already have credibility and what you need to do to gain credibility. This obvious legitimacy will aid in the development of trust and an online following, as well as more leads and higher-paying clients. Finally, consider what your own brand objectives are. Your particular brand purpose and strategy will take shape as a result of your individual aims. Increase business brand awareness, generate more leads, grow your professional network, leverage more media, press, or industry collaborations, monetize your digital presence, and simply open the door to more opportunities like public speaking or a publishing deal are some of the most popular personal brand goals. As you begin to answer all of these questions with pen to paper or fingers to keyboard, your brand foundation will begin to take shape.

These are the social media best practises that everyone should adhere to, regardless of the business they are in or the objectives they have. No "one magical approach" to use social media for marketing that is successful for everyone exists. But everyone can make a few common mistakes. These vary from public relations disasters to simpler, more innocent errors, such as publishing the same information across all platforms.

You can't grow a following without understanding who you're attempting to attract, which is why understanding your audience it's number one on the list. Look closely at the following inquiries:

- Just who are your clients?
- What websites do they frequent?
- How do they get a job?
- What are they concerned with?
- They already know you, right?
- How do they perceive you?
- Do you want them to think that?
- What information must they observe in order to think your goods or services are worthwhile?

That's only the beginning. Make sure thorough audience research is part of your social media marketing strategy. Make a note of it so that everyone on your team is aware of who the target audience is. There's more to defining your target audience than their demographics or a cursory buyer persona. Include their inspirations, pain issues, and reasons why they should choose you as the answer.

You don't have to use every platform to be successful, so don't just download the hottest new app because everyone else is. When establishing a new account, ask:

- Have I got the time—or does my team—to produce quality content for a new platform?
- Does this platform's goal align with my brand?
- Does this audience stay for a while?

You will always be better off concentrating on producing intelligent content for fewer channels rather than releasing generic stuff on all of them. Keep up with the latest social media trends, but be sure to think things through before acting. Oh, hey, with this thorough, free Social Trends 2022 study, we've done all the research for you.

Set objectives, develop a content plan, avoid creating a Insta account just to take part in Dance Like a Chicken Day, etc. Simply put, use strategy in every move you make. An extension of your brand is your content. Like any other aspect of doing business, social media requires careful planning, SMART objectives, and ongoing tactical modifications.

Your fan base is expanding. Your conversion rates are through the roof. You often receive DMs and comments from devoted, enthusiastic clients. Your ideas are on fire. Yes, life is good. No! Yes, the present situation is favourable, but do you understand why? What actually produced these outstanding outcomes? While being fortunate is fantastic, recognising why your material worked well (or not) will help you develop repeatable procedures for effective campaigns. Conduct a recurring social media assessment. Try uploading content at various times and on various days. Ask your audience what they want by conducting a survey. Don't be like Melvin of the Last Minute. A recipe for burnout is coming up with material just before you have to upload it. Planning your social media material gives you the freedom to produce high-quality content, logically organise campaigns (both organic and sponsored), and solicit team input and participation. An automatic Twitter retweet of a Facebook post is not a content strategy. It goes without saying that you can and should repurpose content across several platforms, but the essential word here is "repurposing." Turn the article's main points into a Twitter thread instead of just posting a link to it on all of your social media profiles. Make a YouTube video with a script based on the blog post; in the video description, include a link to the article.

To encourage your followers to read the article in its entirety on your website, stand in front of your phone and film an Instagram reel while pointing to various text sections. It's not necessary to create a thread, reel, tiktok, video material, carousel postings, etc. It's acceptable to distribute links on occasion. However, try to reuse as much of your information as you can. You'll be able to produce more more quickly.

Don't expect to build a loyal following by employing impersonal marketing techniques. To foster meaningful conversation and generate visitors that may really convert, adapt your content to the strengths of each social media site.

Despite seeming like fancy marketing jargon, social listening is basically free, in-the-moment market research. Basic listening searches social media platforms for mentions of your brand, goods, rivals, and certain any other item you wish to look for. Modern techniques can assess brand emotion, identify trademarks in photos, and more. This gives you the inside scoop on what customers truly think of your business or the qualities they desire in a product. But knowledge on its own is insufficient. It must be used in practise. Keep an eye out for daily questions about your sector or requests for suggestions on social media with your AI, then join the conversation with a comment or retweet.

Social listening is effective for developing new products and positioning as well as for major strategic issues. Ben & Jerry's discovered that customers preferred to eat their ice cream curled up inside on a wet day as opposed to outside in the sun by monitoring brand mentions. Social listening is excellent, but you should also make an effort to interact with your audience personally. Inquire about their thoughts and views or ask them amusing questions to learn more about them. You may invite people to leave a comment with their answer, link to an online survey from your social media profiles, or conduct a brief poll on Twitter or Instagram Stories. Create an online community and establish relationships because that is the main goal of social media. Not all feedback is about a product's features.

Customers are texting you or leaving comments on your social media posts with customer care queries in addition to tagging you in a post. Especially if your posts receive hundreds of comments, it is easy to overlook those significant remarks. Mark DMs and comments that need an immediate reply. Regardless of the technology you use, make sure you have a system in place for allocating discussions to maintain order and provide the quickest response times. When most of your customers want the same information, providing good customer service might take a lot of time.

There is a difference between a few unfavourable remarks and a full-fledged PR catastrophe. Regardless of whether the criticism you face is justified or not, you need to have a crisis management strategy in place.

- Who will take the lead on your team's response?
- What will your reaction be?

- Will you announce it to the public?
- Will you reply to each comment individually or will you refer readers to a written statement?
- Will you alter the rule or practise that has enraged people? If so, how will you make that known?

The fact that each platform has different requirements for image or video size or character count is only one of the many reasons you shouldn't cross-post the same material on several platforms. Numerous social networking applications are available to assist with design chores. If you don't have a design staff, Canva or Adobe Express make making visuals simple. Not only are prompt responses valued, but they are also expected. 83% of clients worldwide anticipate a social media reaction within 24 hours, while 28% expect one within an hour. Whether we like it or not, social media continues to set standards that companies must meet if they want to stay competitive.

Even if you don't post every day, make sure someone on your team logs in to reply to comments and direct messages and scan for spam. This will not only preserve your options for prospective usage in the future, but it will also stop potential imposters from using your brand name to pretend to be you. Create an account even if you don't intend to use the site to safeguard your identity and intellectual property. Think it won't happen to you? Think again. It even happens to celebrities. Scammers built up phoney Twitter profiles with usernames that were one letter off from those of genuine, renowned businesses in 2020, and they managed to defraud individuals out of $80 million.

With a new year upon us, we've prepared a guide to assist businesses in succeeding across all social networks in the ever-changing world of social media marketing. For businesses of all shapes and sizes, sectors, and target audiences, social media is a key component of digital marketing. To benefit from their social channels, companies must stay current with the most recent advancements and changes in the industry, which are always changing due to upgrades and new releases.

Around the world, 3.5 billion users of social media networks are predicted by 2023. That amounts to about 40% of the world's population. Given such numbers, it's hardly surprising that companies invest so much time and energy on social media marketing.If you're just beginning your adventure into social media marketing, I suggest you look through our Social Media Marketing Glossary for a comprehensive set of terminology that will keep you current with all the lingo! Find out the best strategies on how to boost your personal brand?

A personal brand needs to appropriately represent your personal and professional identity in order to grow. Knowing who you are will help you do this. Concentrate on you. Consider your advantages and disadvantages.

In contrast to the past, you no longer require an agency to gain attention. There is schmoozing and an ascent up the celebrity ladder. These days, increasing your influence comes first. Social media makes it simple to gain notice and expand your online presence. Consider the following queries:

- What areas am I the best at?
- What traits do I possess that others find admirable?
- Which assignments have I struggled with and sought assistance with? Which role drains my energy the most?
- What initiatives pique my attention the most?

You may seek assistance from your family, friends, and coworkers if you are having trouble responding to these questions, advises Chris Coleman of RV Talk. Ask them to sum you up. You will be able to brand your many personality traits once you are more conscious of them. Because they don't want to limit themselves, many people find it difficult to select a specialization. Consider specialising because, as your profession develops, your personal brand will evolve. The ideal approach is to focus on a certain region and watch it develop over time.

A personal brand, goes beyond who you are today; it is a strategy of where you want to go. You should evaluate your strengths and weaknesses in relation to the sector or job you wish to succeed in when you have a firm awareness of your current abilities and competences. Work out the details of your narrative before you tell it. It is crucial to have a strong grasp of your unique brand identity and personality. The following essential components should be included in your personal brand framework: This should address your "why" in terms of brand purpose. What do you hope to accomplish?

- Nowadays, brands place a greater emphasis on values. and so must your own brand. What do you wish to represent? What is most important in your personal and professional life?Make an effort to identify at least five key values.
- A brand should be explicit about the psychological and practical advantages it offers consumers. You may contribute to personal branding with both your hard and soft abilities. Coaching, mentoring, writing, public speaking, and other examples of hard talents include soft skills, which include open-mindedness, fast

thinking, independence, and others.

- A brand's name, logo, colours, and typefaces are examples of physical branding aspects. According to David Morgan, proprietor of the e-commerce company Snorkel-Mart, your personal brand should be the colours and design components you utilise across all of your social media platforms.

David goes on to say that you should emphasise your unique selling points in order to distinguish your own brand. It is known as a company's USP, or unique selling proposition. Your individuality should be the focus of your personal branding, along with your USP.

- Prior to developing your brand, you need also identify the target market you hope to attract. It might include recruiters, businesses, and individuals in addition to thought leaders in the field. To create an appropriate tale, you must understand your audience. It will also decide how your narrative is presented.
- You must comprehend the industry you want to work in before you can begin to plan your career. Find authorities in this field and pay attention to them. Find out where they contribute their thinking rather than stopping there. Find successful people and study their methods.

Try contacting these folks for an informational interview while you make a list of the organisations you want to work for and the business executives who inspire you. To learn more about your chosen field, pose the following questions:

- How did you break into the field?
- What actions have you taken to complete the transition?
- What do you think the industry will look like in 10 years?
- How do you stay current with fashion?

Informational interviews are advantageous since you may learn about the business while also promoting yourself. This is already enhancing your brand.

Create a 30- to 60-second tale about yourself as you conceptualise your own brand. This will be useful when going to an event or casual party because it will be simple to briefly describe oneself. Your elevator pitch ought to accurately portray your skills. Limit your points to the aspects of yourself that you wish to emphasise.

To expand your professional network, I advise frequently and successfully lifting your network, similar to lifting weights at a gym. By consistently participating in official and informal networking events, you may establish connections with the appropriate individuals, such as colleagues and thought leaders in your field.
You may provide more value to interactions the more connections you have with other people. Because people will know your brand, you will benefit more.

The simplest and most powerful strategy to establish your personal brand is to get someone to recommend you because they will let others know how valuable you are. This is comparable to building customer testimonials and reviews in sales and marketing. Additionally, you must grow your own reviews through referrals.

In the modern digital era, customers may easily locate your company online. That is the extent of the internet's power. Therefore, why not use it? Create a website on your own. Make it tidy and more attentive to the services you provide. In order to connect with your client on a more personal level, your website serves as your online business card.

In addition to a website, having a strong social media presence will keep your viewers interested and encourage them to recommend your company to others. Your pitch may reach a bigger audience by using social media sites like Facebook, Twitter, Instagram, TikTok, and Linkedin.

You should boost your social media presence by publishing interesting content like photographs, videos, blog entries, and many others. On certain systems, a call-to-action is implemented via the add buttons. It may aid in improving communications and boosting engagement. Posting images instead of simple phrases might help you receive more attention.

Your personal brand is always changing in line with the digital ecology. Don't put yourself in a box. To network with new people, cultivate your career, and meet new individuals, alter your character. Don't be reluctant to build a brand that makes you stand out. Keep your unique selling proposition in mind while you build your own brand. Emphasize your personal goals, special interests, and principles.

Emma Watson, an actress best known for her part in the Harry Potter film series, has worked hard to change how people perceive her as an adult actor who places a significant emphasis on activism. Emma is truly highly committed to the feminist movement in addition to her acting profession. In order to become a UN Women Goodwill Ambassador, she was able to reinvent herself as a strong female leader who sought education outside of acting. She also moderated panel discussions for the COP26 and promoted eco-friendly fashion.Her goals are clear, and social responsibility is at the centre of her personal philosophy.

Elon Musk has established a number of companies, including SpaceX and Tesla Motors. He's been compared to "real-life Tony Stark" because of his unconventional thinking. He has developed a strong personal brand that is associated with success thanks to his rather unconventional demeanour.

The drawbacks of this line of employment are becoming increasingly obvious to the millions of people who in some way commercialise their online presence, especially at a time when so many people are reevaluating their professional paths. The line between a personal brand and a profession becomes more hazy. Families are put under stress. It asks that every private moment be mined for useful information.

Everyone is aware of the importance of good branding in business. Here are some strategies to improve your personal brand in 2022. Like Nike, its "Just Do It" catchphrase has come to represent the company. You will recognise it even if you don't see the logo. It establishes the tone for how a business communicates with the public and presents itself to them. A company's branding may be seen in its goods, staff, values, and other aspects of the business.

A successful brand stands out from the crowd, generating greater exposure and revenue while also improving the consumer experience. You may not be aware, but branding is not limited to businesses. Additionally, experts may contribute their knowledge, abilities, objectives, and tales. Having a personal brand is no longer a nice-to-have in an increasingly digital world. It is essential.

Are you prepared?

First, educate your current team, clients, or executives by articulating your worth on a regular basis. Let them know what you like doing the most, why you're good at it, and how they can use your skills to their benefit. Consider how beneficial having access to this information would be for your coworkers, superiors, and managers. They aim to place you on projects that will highlight your abilities. They want you to be the team's most productive and efficient member. Understanding your worth is a terrific approach to get started. It's valuable to them, and it's valuable to you as well. Imagine heading into work tomorrow with a day packed with fascinating duties and projects that will allow you to shine. You get to show off your skills while also feeling recognised and cherished. And you're genuinely kept in the loop when new possibilities surface that are ideal for you.

Wouldn't that be incredible?

When you communicate your worth, you put yourself in a position to perform the things you're not only skilled at but also enjoy. It's easier to position yourself for chances that are suitable for you when people appreciate your talents, influence, and worth. Finally, remember that establishing your personal brand's base is communicating your value. In today's environment, hiring managers pay close attention to your prospective social effect or cultural fit. People aren't only looking for the best worker for the job. They seek the best candidate for the job who also has the necessary qualifications. You are your own brand, with your own personality, abilities, and stories. Branding is no longer limited to businesses and products. And the value you provide, or what you bring to the table, is a significant element of that brand. Here are some illustrations of some of the top branding websites for you to be inspired by.

Making an identity for a person or a company is referred to as "personal branding." Personal branding is similar to creating a set of values and domain knowledge around an individual or group of organisations that they can identify with. A person's appearance, mannerisms, and actions all contribute to their personal brand. Whatever your area of expertise, having a strong personal brand can make it easier to stand out in a crowded market. In the modern era of ever-changing trends and technology, having the correct personal branding may help you stand out. Here is all the information you want regarding personal branding. The most effective personal brands are developed by individuals with specialised expertise acquired through experience in a certain field. Creating a personal brand is intended to benefit people in the most genuine way possible. Given that we operate in an attention economy, many people could use some insightful advice from those who have already done the job. There's a good chance that if you've worked on a pitch for a while, you've learned a lot.

Tony Robbins is a controversial yet well-known figure. American author, businessman, philanthropist, and life coach Anthony Jay Robbins (often known as Tony Robbins) is the author of several incredible books like Unlimited Power, Awaken the Giant Within, and others. If you've been interested in leadership, business, or personal branding, you've definitely seen or heard of Tony Robbins before. His lectures are well-known, and he routinely travels to various parts of the world to provide infomercials and seminars to uplift people. Tony Robbins is interested in our motivations for acting in certain ways. His self-financed personal brand permeates all of his books, seminars, podcasts, and other media. People pay attention to him since he is one of the well-known faces and because of his charm and boundless energy. The website for Tony Robbins is a fantastic illustration of effective personal branding. The homepage of the website is rather straightforward, has a dark colour scheme, and lists all of Tony Robbins' services. There is a large photograph of him and his crowd as well, which perfectly demonstrates how well-liked he is.

Thanks to Tony Robbins' prolific output of books, seminars, and other content, it would be difficult to find someone who is unfamiliar with him and his style of financial self-help, whether they love him or hate him. Of course, we must not overlook his charm, his dynamism, and his stunning smile. If you haven't been following him, your mind may still see Tony from the 1990s, strutting around in front of his adoring supporters in all his loud, exuberant grandeur. But as things changed, so did his identity. He has become more refined and restrained and is no longer yelling at full blast. His current website positions him as a financial instructor for the contemporary environment rather than the raucous self-help guru of the past.

Tony wears business clothing to match the site's dark colour scheme, making him appear more like an IT worker than a yelling prophet of self-empowerment. Melyssa Griffin defines her mission as helping "heart-centered high achievers grow their income and impact online." This summary communicates who she is, appeals to entrepreneurial aspirations, and connects on an emotional level. His website showcases a personal brand that is contemporary and relevant, eschewing the flash and pizzaz of the past.

You undoubtedly know Pat Flynn if you're interested in affiliate marketing or internet marketing. He is an American businessman, well-known blogger, and host of the "Smart Passive Income" podcast and blog, which offers advice on how to launch a successful internet venture. The only thing that comes to mind when we hear the name Pat Flynn is honesty. It's clear from his material that Pat Flynn is ruthlessly honest (be it videos, podcasts, or articles). In addition, he does not hold anything back when discussing how to create a successful website or internet company. He is so well-liked in the world of blogging because of this.

It is well known that Aaron Ward sells and teaches about marketing digital products. He has a blog where he offers advice to others on how to build their companies and is an active YouTuber. The homepage and the remainder of Ward's website have a contemporary look. Among the sea of content producers, his website and presence stand out, drawing viewers to his work. Entrepreneur Aaron Ward is passionate about assisting creators in producing and marketing digital goods online. At the centre of his personal brand is a gorgeous portfolio website, developed in Webflow. His website highlights some of the businesses he has worked with, including Medium, Red Bull, and

Spotify. Aaron teaches individuals how to develop their own brands on social media through his blog and YouTube channel. Aaron stands out in a sea of personal brands because of a wonderful fusion of personality and content production, providing him the opportunity to develop into a thought leader in the social media sphere.

One of the most well-known bloggers and the top SEO specialist in the world is Neil Patel. Neil is a co-founder of many significant online businesses, including Crazy Egg, Hello Bar, and KISSmetrics. He also runs the blog NeilPatel.com, where he offers advice on how to increase search traffic to a website or an online store. Neil aids Fortune 500 firms like Amazon, NBC, GM, HP, and Viacom in increasing their total sales and earnings. Additionally, he publishes a tonne of information on his blogs and contributes as a guest writer to well-known blogs like Forbes, Inc., and others. Being everywhere is the most important lesson Neil Patel wants you to take away. Neil is a prominent blogger. Neil has a blog for himself. Neil publishes podcasts. Neil gives workshops all around the world. In order to create successful internet enterprises, Neil conducts webinars and interviews people. Neil takes numerous different actions to develop and expand his brand.

Kyle Andre Hunter, nicknamed K, Sparks is a musician, songwriter, and performer. His website is a personal branding mecca. He offers everything pertaining to his brand, including songs, beats, "behind the scenes," and musical ideas. The K. Sparks' website features a portrait image as well as a menu that directs visitors to his body of work. The website's information is concise and pertinent. K. A fantastic example of a company leveraging its brand as a portfolio is Sparks.

Journalist Libby Peterson works in New York. Libby Peterson's website does not emphasise her photographs, in contrast to the other personal branding websites on this list. Libby Peterson's website's homepage is vibrant, and her portfolio is prominently displayed for everyone to see.

Photographer and storyteller Louise Amelia Whitehouse The website has several images that Louise Amelia Whitehouse took all around the world. The website's clean, appealing appearance also gives visitors a lasting impression of the author's works.

Lewis David Howes, better known by his stage name Lewis Howes, is an American author, businessman, and well-known podcaster. He is the author of the book "The School of Greatness." Thousands of marketers across the world listen to Lewis' The School of Greatness podcast, which he presents together with his blog of the same name. Lewis was also a former professional football player for the Arena League. The most important thing to take away from Lewis Howes is to strive to be a better version of yourself. Every day, work on your physical, mental, and emotional well-being. We all have the chance to learn something new every day, and by concentrating on improving yourself, you may motivate others to do the same. The secret to success is that.

Graphic designer and YouTuber Alice Thorpe Her YouTube channel is a great resource for learning graphic design, but her sense of humour and upbeat attitude also keep her audience interested and help to build her brand. Thorpe's YouTube account and her website both include vibrant artwork. According to the "Stumbling Through" section of her YouTube bio, it is what her branding stands for. That is what her branding portrays, as indicated in her YouTube bio: "Stumbling through life one pixel at a time."

Moreover, her website highlights her popular lessons, which are quite helpful.

Alice Thorpe defines herself on her YouTube channel as a "freelance graphic designer bumbling through life one pixel at a time." Alice isn't hesitant to poke fun at herself, and her self-referential slogan is a fantastic beginning. On YouTube and her own website, she creates a tonne of stuff geared toward designers. She is the type of expert who never addresses her audience with subservience. Alice creates engaging material by fusing her professional knowledge with her informal, humorous manner.

Nesha Woolery's website welcomes us with "Hey designer woman!" — speaking directly to the demographic she wishes to attract. Alice does a terrific job of continually conveying her personality via all of her amazing material, much like those major businesses. Nesha provides online classes, videos, and articles for women in design and has experience in project management and organising. She provides a specialised service to a certain demographic with a bright, airy style that ties in with the look of her own personal brand.

Gary is generally recognised for converting his family's liquor business into one of the top e-commerce websites. He is active on all social media sites, including Facebook, Instagram, and YouTube. His humble beginning to a prosperous life serves as the foundation of his personal brand. On the homepage of his official website, yellow, black, and white colours are used to highlight, among other things, his accomplishments, blog, and offerings.

Bill Nye, sometimes referred to as "the Science Guy," had a long and fruitful career. His comedy and dad jokes, which all feature Nye's personal branding, serve to impart information. His official website opens with a science quotation to welcome visitors, and the remaining pages are a combination of his comic- and science-inspired homepage. All of these properly capture Bill Nye's unique branding. People will trust you if you have a strong identity. We choose name-brand items over generic ones at the shop because we are aware of what we are obtaining. There are none. The product's value and selling factors are proven and well-known. Equally recognised should be your own brand. Underneath the surface of his widespread popularity, Bill Nye is a man who values fostering a greater understanding and respect for science. He may be renowned for his bowties and scientific dad jokes. As crucial to his personal brand as his talents as an entertainer are his zeal for reason and critical thought. He portrays the amiable, silly geek on stage. His mechanical engineering training transforms him from a TV personality blowing up test tubes full of vibrant liquids to a respected authority. Despite the fact that his website advertises his books and online shop, the majority of the information is science-related and understandable, even for individuals who have never put on a lab coat. It's challenging to know who to believe in a world populated by SEO "experts" who claim to have the ability to boost your website's traffic by 100% in a couple of weeks.

Marie's website is a fantastic illustration of effective personal branding. She is a well-known person and businesswoman with followers in more than 200 nations. Her hip website has a portfolio on the front page. Even if the homepage is jam-packed with events, Marie's personality is well captured by the appropriately optimised design. Marie Forleo's business school, B-School, is an excellent example of advertising on the homepage of a website, as it features success stories of its students on its homepage.

One of the best-known YouTubers and an early pioneer of the vlogging movement is Casey Neistat. His personal branding, "Do what you can't," personifies his straightforward website. The colour scheme and layout of his website are rather straightforward, frequently pointing visitors to the most engaging pages and messaging.

Billie Eilish's website accurately portrays her unique branding. The website tries many different forms of material, much like she does with her music. Billie's music, videos, and personalised merchandise are all featured on the homepage.

In the tech sector, Nicholas is well known, particularly in the field of digital marketing. He is an author, trainer, and Facebook advertising expert. The homepage of his website includes customer endorsements, a link to his free and paid training, as well as videos and images of him grinning widely. Nicholas's personal brand—a happy guy with a successful background in digital marketing—is the result of all of this.

Another well-known self-help expert and author is Tim Ferriss. He provides a variety of courses, including Ferriss's own brand, for this purpose. He focuses on altering the mindsets of companies and employees. His website's homepage has a straightforward blog along with additional products and connections to his podcasts. American author, entrepreneur, and public speaker Timothy Ferriss (sometimes known as Tim Ferriss) is the author of some of the best-selling books, including The 4-Hour Workweek and The 4-Hour Body. What can Tim Ferriss teach us? Tim Ferriss is a true example. He has a net worth in the millions and was an early investor in firms with billion-dollar valuations, including Facebook, Twitter, Uber, and others. Tim is skilled at creating a brand through book authoring. He has published several self-help books, and because to his incredible marketing abilities, practically every one of them becomes a worldwide bestseller right away. He also hosts "The Tim Ferriss Show," which has been ranked #1 out of more than 300,000 podcasts and is one of the most popular on Apple Podcasts. Millions of people worldwide download it. Tim Ferriss can teach you how to network effectively. He travels the world to meet creative individuals, broadcasts a podcast, and conducts numerous interviews. Start networking like Tim Ferriss if you truly want to develop like him.

According to Mel Abraham's website, he is a well-known businessman, author, and trainer. Abraham's supporters often attend his lectures in large numbers. Speaking with confidence and using his own voice are key components of Mel Abraham's personal branding. Mel's website features a fresh colour scheme of white and yellow with black accents. His work, a link to his training, and videos from his YouTube channel are all included on the homepage. You may access the most recent podcast by clicking on the window at the top of the website.

Mark Manson is a well-known online celebrity and the author of several best-selling books. Because he writes without any filters, which is popular, Manson is able to reach more than one million people each month through his blog and YouTube channel. His writing career began with blogs, which he ultimately transitioned into books. Manson's personal branding is heavily influenced by his straightforward explanations of self-help topics. His website is straightforward, with a blog for the public and a button that may be clicked to subscribe. You may select one of his free ebooks by clicking on an icon with an intriguing topic. Mark Manson is an online entrepreneur and author of a best-selling book. Mark has established an outstanding personal brand for himself, reaching over one million people every month through his website and blog. Due to the fact that Mark originally began building a following on his blog, he is a fantastic example of a personal brand done well. His blog's readership adored the self-improvement books he eventually published, which helped him become a best-selling author and climb the bestseller lists. With the popularity of his books, Mark also developed a subscription service—another way of monetising his website. Additionally, he expanded to other social media sites like YouTube and began producing material on subjects he had previously covered in books and blog postings.

Copywriting is Gari Cruze's forte, and it is also his brand. And his website explains why he is so good at it. The homepage greets viewers with images and, when hovered over, displays the campaigns he worked on. It is a fantastic personal branding strategy that enables clients to become acquainted with Gari Cruze's work.

Australian surfer and 10-time champion Sean O'Brien is the face of his website. Despite being brief, the website satisfies all the criteria for a top personal branding website. The webpage for Brien is up-to-date and animated. One of the greatest websites for personal branding was created, including the site's logo, text, and content.

Charli Marie is a contemporary designer, author, and YouTuber. The spirit of personal branding is perfectly encapsulated in her official website. With services appearing for the public, the website has a purple and white style. People may learn about Charli Marie's expertise and the projects she has been working on by visiting her website. That is the ideal illustration of a personal brand executed well. When Charli Marie launched a Tumblr devoted to the pop punk band Fall Out Boy, she was a design student. Love for the band and a desire to connect with other like-minded fans led to the creation of this fan page. Her T-shirt line was created as a result of her Tumblr success. Writing on the success and failure of her t-shirt company, Charli She frames it as a crucial milestone in her development as a designer rather than focusing on the momentum her firm lost. Charli's Tumblr tale encourages action for individuals who have creative ideas that seem to be only for fun since you never know what opportunities a fan page for your favourite pop punk band will present. Today, Charli runs a popular YouTube channel, works remotely for Convertkit, and has built a life filled with travel and enjoyment. Her personal brand is heavily reliant on her positive outlook and design abilities. She offers yet another excellent illustration of the fact that there are several routes to achievement.

Billie Eilish combines awkwardness and hubris in equal measure. Within the first 10 seconds of an interview, she can be both irritating and endearing.While still adhering to mainstream ideals, her music toes the border of experimentalism. Her own website embodies this mood with a combination of design elements, including handwritten notes, hazy photographs, script typography, and glamorous images of Billie. Her distinctive quirks are virtually anti-brand; they let people quickly identify her music and aesthetic.

As part of her own brand, Martha Stewart has a wide range of interests, including cooking, designing, and gardening. Her website is clean and comprises grey and white hues with black typography. The webpage is crammed with a lot of stuff for her viewers.

Casey Neistat's website is designed with whitespace and a few outbound links because he's "not entirely sure what purpose a website would serve someone like me, so this page is here to redirect you to more interesting places." Casey's films are sufficient to convey his own brand of rebellion thanks to his large social media following and over 11 million YouTube subscribers. He is obviously motivated by intelligence and instinct. He has spent his whole career exceeding expectations and defying those who have told him he can't achieve anything. He's a vlogger (video blogger), started the media firm Beme, and has gotten recognition from big-name sources like Forbes. He lives by the motto "Do what you can't," has spent his life fighting the critics, and has overcome adversity via force. His material is brazen and unrepentant. He exhorts his listeners to pursue their goals without holding back.

Mindy Kaling is a well-known personality who dabbles in acting, writing, and producing, among other things. Her personal brand is heavily influenced by her sense of humour and humorous timing, which her website expertly conveys. Sky blue and white are blended to create a contemporary homepage. The written content on the website is humorous and lighthearted, perfectly encapsulating Mindy Kaling's brand. We've all laughed a lot thanks to Mindy Kaling's work as a writer, performer, and producer. She has made a name for herself as a writer of witty humour that subverts Hollywood and accepted social mores. Her personal brand encompasses more than just categorising her as a writer, feminist, or actress. Even though Mindy is excellent in many different ways, her brand gives a clear indication of who she is and what is important to her.

With a readership of more than 600,000 readers each month, Adam is well-known in the blogging world. Adam approaches his blog as a company, adopting similar strategies and getting inspiration from others. His website is simple, listing all of Enfroy's services that make him a brand.

The actor and writer Lior Raz is most known for producing the television series "Fauda," and his one-page website brilliantly captures what acting is all about. The homepage of Lior Raz's website displays his images with various subjects that scroll around and change.

JR Taylor is a well-known choreographer who has experience working with a number of well-known celebrities, including Jennifer Lopez and Beyonce. The JR Taylor personal website perfectly captures the essence of his dance. The major component of his website features goods and dancing performances.

Blogger Adam Enfroy has built up a following of more than 500,000 readers per month in the short time since he first established his own brand. Adam's credo is to "blog like a startup," and he uses the same startup marketing techniques to create his own personal website. Adam is certainly an inspiration when it comes to how he tackles personal branding. Adam demonstrates how quickly a personal brand can develop by treating blogging like a company. Adam is a terrific role model to follow if you're thinking about launching a blog for your own brand. Adam demonstrates how quickly a personal brand can develop by treating blogging like a company. Adam is a terrific role model to follow if you're thinking about launching a blog for your own brand. Adam demonstrates through his income reports how he generates seven figures just from his personal brand. Adam is able to monetise his site through affiliate money, sponsorship revenue, and course purchases since he built a following through SEO blogging.

David Milan is a skilled 3D designer and artist who has created work for a number of prestigious brands and well-known people. His website is a work of art in and of itself. What could be more effective than presenting your portfolio as original artwork? His personality is displayed to the public through the website's material, which is full of original designs.

Author, physician, and campaigner, Dr. Gilbert Simon. His website has a simple layout and effectively employs the accent colours of white, black, and light blue. Simon's website's home page features examples of his work, a connection to his YouTube channel, and an Amazon link for ordering his book. A simple yet powerful website highlights Gilbert Simon's brand's beliefs, vision, and offerings.

American businessman, author, speaker, and online sensation Gary Vaynerchuk has millions of followers across social media platforms including Instagram, Facebook, YouTube, and others. Gary is well known for being a wine critic who helped his family's wine company expand from $3 million to $60 million. Gary also understands how to develop his own brand and take it to the next level in order to create an internet empire. Really like what you do and smash it: If you want to be successful at anything, enjoy doing it and the same thing applies for building your brand and bringing your business to the next level. Gary consistently teaches through his videos and Instagram stories that if you love what you do for a living, you'll be able to succeed in business and motivate others. Gary Vaynerchuk, like many individuals with a strong personal brand, has a fascinating origin story: he transformed the family liquor company into an online retail behemoth. In Gary's case, perseverance and hard work let him rise from poor beginnings to prosperity. He epitomises self-determinism and sincerity. He presents himself as a realist who wants you to succeed on your own terms when he posts information on websites like YouTube, Instagram, and LinkedIn. In addition, he helped create VaynerMedia.

Elon Musk is the creator of the Boring Company, SpaceX, and Tesla. His goals are to do things that have never been done before. Because of this strategy, he became the most recognisable brand and the richest individual. People pay attentive attention to what you have to say when you're a well-known person, which Elon Musk expertly makes use of. In addition to being active on social media, Musk engages the audience at seminars or live sessions, and his fans like his sense of humour.

Elon Musk became well-known not only for his talking but also for consistently delivering on his promises. Whether it was a fully automated vehicle, reusable rockets, or a satellite that offers extremely fast internet, Musk succeeded in doing what many people said was not feasible. People trust a brand more if it delivers on its promises rather than just making them. No matter how effective your personal brand is currently, a lack of consistency may destroy it. Elon Musk became the brand he is today due to his never-ending pursuit of things or solutions that were previously unthinkable. No matter how well-known or successful your brand is, there comes a time when people start looking forward to the next thing. Humans are naturally on the lookout for novel experiences. Elon Musk has a complete understanding of it. What he is today is the consequence of his ongoing new ideas and their implementation.

If you've ever looked up sales training on YouTube, you'll be familiar with Grant Cardone and his work. He is the best-selling author of several amazing books, including 10X Rule, the world's #1 sales trainer, a well-known public speaker, an influential figure on social media globally, and a real estate tycoon with a fortune in the hundreds of millions of dollars. Despite having a "below average" upbringing, Grant Cardone has accomplished incredible things and raised his net worth to more than $300 million. Grant is the top example of a self-brand statement in our list of the top 10, for this reason. The rest is history; he amassed enormous wealth through real estate, began penning amazing books on sales training, conducted sales seminars, launched a YouTube channel, launched his own TV programme, and realised his long-held ambition of living a 10x life. Grant makes it a point to produce at least one YouTube video every week that discusses either sales, inspiration, company, or money, despite his hectic schedule. So, if you want to advance in life, perform and think at 10x levels, and be reliable in whatever you do. Get up! You won't be saved by anyone. There won't be someone to look after your family or your retirement. If there is one lesson Grant Cardone left us with, it is to think really big. After graduating, Grant began working as a salesperson. He saved every cent he made until he was ready to put all of his earnings into real estate. There won't be someone "making things work out" for you. Utilising every second of every day at 10X levels is the only way to do this.

Do you remember the popular Ted Talk titled "Your body language affects who you are?" Amy Cuddy, a social psychologist and associate professor at Harvard Business School, demonstrates how to use digital networks, online resources, and a strong offline presence to increase one's potential success and scope of influence. When one uses technology to share their work with a larger audience, they may achieve great things, as Amy is a shining example of the heights one's work may reach when using technologies to reach a wider audience.

Most people can appreciate when something is truly sincere. The CEO of LinkedIn, Jeff Weiner, is approachable despite his position. I only need to go to this great piece that just happened to pop up in my LinkedIn feed, where he describes how his profession developed to become what it is now. By remaining active on social networks like LinkedIn and sharing stuff like this, Jeff establishes a reputation with regular people. Be aware that a strong personal brand is also shaped by a strong LinkedIn profile. I'll recommend you to the maestro himself for an excellent example of a LinkedIn profile!

The British entrepreneur, investor, and philanthropist Sir Richard Charles Nicholas Branson, also known as Richard Branson, is the author of numerous best-selling books, including Screw It, Let's Do It! Unquestionably, one of the finest role models for self-branding in 2022 is Richard Branson. Richard is renowned for launching the Virgin Group, which has influence over more than 400 businesses worldwide. He runs his company at a completely new level and motivates millions of employees with his management style. If you don't care about people first, you just can't generate money. I've never been rewarded for choosing money above compassion, and I've subsequently discovered that how well you treat your audience affects how much money you make. Pat Flynn, Will It Fly? Here are some things you may learn about developing your own brand from him. Become a go-getter;

an example of someone who exemplifies this trait is Richard Branson. He takes a huge financial risk .If he really wants to achieve something. Whether or not you know it, Richard Branson founded his airline, Virgin Atlantic, in 1984 as a result of the cancellation of his trip from Puerto Rico to the Virgin Islands. He chartered an aircraft, borrowed a chalk, and, as a joke, scribbled "Virgin Airlines" on the blackboard's top, along with the words "$39 one way to BVI," instead of waiting for the next available flight. He set out to gather up every passenger who had been rescheduled, and then he loaded his first aircraft. Virgin Atlantic is the second-largest airline in the UK, three decades after its founding. Therefore, if you have a belief in anything, just go for it and don't listen to or imitate others. Don't allow failure to be an option, and don't let failure scare you. Make it happen by putting everything you have into it. The secret to success is that. You cannot gain anything if you don't take any risks. That's all there is to it.

"I can really state that I have never started a business with the intention of making money alone. If that is the primary purpose, then I feel you are better off not doing it."- Richard Branson

Author Simon Oliver Sinek, also known as Simon Sinek, is a British-American who has written four books, the best-selling of which is "Start With Why." He is a well-known consultant as well as a motivational speaker who covers leadership and business topics. Unbeknownst to you, more than 40 million people have viewed his TEDx lecture on "How exceptional leaders take action," and over 20 million have watched it on YouTube. In his TED presentation, Simon Sinek discusses a straightforward yet effective framework for inspiring leadership that begins with a golden circle and the question "Why?" He gives examples of Apple, Martin Luther King, and the Wright brothers to illustrate his point. Communicate your goal clearly. Simon Sinek began evangelising "Start with why" in 2009 and has been aggressively teaching others about it ever since. People like Simon Sinek place enormous pressure on those who attend his seminars, webinars, TED presentations, and other events to discover their purpose, or "why." Knowing your why and beginning to express your future vision clearly can help you build your personal brand and take it to the next level.

"If you hire individuals only based on their ability to perform a task, they will work for your money. However, if you employ individuals who share your beliefs, they will toil and sweat for you."

An online writer who is the genuine article when it comes to Google SEO, Brian Dean's website establishes him as a respectable authority thanks to its detailed material, real-person endorsements, and lack of shady advertisements. Trust is the cornerstone of his personal brand.

A solid personal branding plan gives professionals the platform, chance, and edge they need to thrive in their industry, build a reputation, and inspire others. Even if that is succinctly stated, developing a successful personal brand requires strategy and perseverance. Although there are many tips and guidelines, nothing puts the subject in perspective like some solid examples of personal branding. What exactly does the finest personal brand look like, after all? Is there such a thing as the ideal personal brand?Perhaps, perhaps not.

The reach of Martha Stewart's brand is so broad. She is an excellent chef, has a keen eye for interior design, is skilled in landscape design, and is capable of handling pretty much any duty involving home aesthetics. Whether she is developing a chicken pasta dish or a colour scheme for a painting, her sense of delicate refinement permeates everything she produces. Whereas some individuals with well-known companies might make a little less of an effort online, Martha makes the complete opposite effort. She is not renowned for being laid-back. The recipes, DIY projects, entertainment suggestions, and other lifestyle-related items on her website are all bursting with her personality. Her brand is still strong today because of her consistent productivity.

What comes to mind when you hear the name Microsoft in a similar way? Bill Gates, I presume? It's referred to as "personal branding." So, what is the significance of building a strong brand? Do you know the identity of Facebook's creator? The majority of people, we wager, are aware that Mark Zuckerberg founded Facebook. Do you, however, know who started Twitter? Most people, in our opinion, are unaware of who he is (who is Jack Dorsey btw). We often use Facebook and Twitter, but the majority of us are unaware of the names of Twitter's CEO and founder.

The reason Mark Zuckerberg is so well-liked is because, in contrast to Jack Dorsey, the founder of Twitter, he has been concentrating on strengthening his total brand. Because of this, more people are familiar with Zuck than Jack. In light of that, the advantages of developing a powerful personal brand are self-branding helps you create trust since people trust other individuals more than they do businesses. It increases your reputation and makes it easier for you to stand out from other rivals in your sector. Self-branding aids in boosting overall growth, sales, and income. Most importantly, you do not need to introduce yourself!

How do you define personal branding? You may create a visionary brand by using self-branding, which is also known as charisma. Steve Jobs is without doubt the finest example of personal branding. What springs to mind when you hear the name Steve Jobs? Apple, yes? Simply put, Steve Jobs came to be associated with the name Apple. Personal branding is necessary, whether you are building an internet empire or a web-based firm. Without establishing oneself as an authority, it is impossible to create a successful website or company. Self-branding has a role in this. This book is just for you if you're seeking for some of the greatest self-brand statement examples and ideas for enhancing your overall branding. We'll be talking about successful people like Elon Musk, Simon Sinek, and Tony Robbins.

"There is no space for being just another name in the throng in the employment market and business environment of today. You must distinguish yourself from the opposition. You must appeal to your target market more, and you may do this by developing a distinctive personal brand."

Nearly every well-known person in the world, including Elon Musk, Mark Zuckerberg, Steve Jobs, and Bill Gates, has their own distinctive personality and way of being. What defines their brand is not the product they created, but rather how each of them interacts with the audience, delivers results, and conducts themselves in front of a large audience. Let's examine Elon Musk's biography in detail to see what we can learn from him, one of the most well-known and wealthy people in the world today. Voice is a crucial component of a brand's identity. Consider the voices behind companies like Progressive, McDonald's, and

Apple; you can certainly see a distinct tone and style for each one. Our understanding of a brand's target audience comes from how they talk to them.

Always keep in mind that youngsters learn to walk by standing up and moving about until they can move independently. Therefore, they fail frequently. Building a personal brand is more of an art than a science. If you want to have a lasting presence in your market, you must identify a distinct need and attempt to address it. Take inspiration and knowledge from the successful personal branding examples of people like Bill Nye, Shaun White, and Charli Marie.

Success is frequently founded on excellent personal branding because it quickly informs us who a person is and where their skill lies. Breaking the rules is one of the finest ways to learn quickly, and failure is frequently the first step toward long-term success.

About The Author

Dr. Amit Das, is a renowned executive advisor, consultant, educationist, author, speaker, counsellor, and coach whose 25+ years of business experience provides high-impact, practical solutions that support his clients' leadership development and organisational transformations. He worked for fortune 500 companies and left rich leagacy of organising transformational learning workshops. He has transformed more than 5000+ working executives through his path breaking capability building learning workshops. Dr. Amit Das is recognised as an innovative, principled thought leader who combines intellectual rigor and discipline with an ability to translate theory into practice. His operational skills are coupled with a strategic ability to analyse, develop, and implement successful strategies for profitability, growth, and sustainability.

Dr. Amit Das has a successful track record in aligning learning and training solutions to key business strategy with a strong focus on flawless execution excellence to facilitate individual, business divisional, and organisational performance. He keeps relentless focus on measuring training impact and ROI, people capability building graphs, training process governance, performance coaching, and strategic thinking. These have been some of his key individual success traits. His core capabilities include performance coaching, designing training and development frameworks, psychometric assessment and analysis, competency framework development and assessments, content design and facilitation of soft skills and leadership programmes, Learning Management Systems, Learning Impact Measurement, Talent Analysis, and Performance Coaching and Counselling.

Dr. Amit Das has authored multiple management and self-development books, like 90 Minutes Mindfulness, Change Your Perspective Change Your Life, The Alchemy Of Resilient Leadership, Redefining Organisational Excellence, High Impact Leadership, Redefining Corporate Spectrum, Create Your Leadership Edge, Love-Laugh- Live With Happiness, SMART Parenting @ Zero Cost, Redefining HRM, Building Organisational Capability, Attomic Attention, Redefining The Power Of Mentoring, Making The Most Future Fit Organisation, Redefining Talent Management, Defining Your Success Factors, Make The Most Of Your Life, Better Half or Bitter Half, Psychology Of Learning And Development, The Transformative Mind & Soul are few of them.

He has a Ph.D. and a Fellowship in strategic learning, along with his first class degrees in Human Resource Management, Marketing Management, International Business, and Corporate Laws from the top business schools in India. He is a certified Psychometric analyst, HR Analyst, OD Interventionist, Human Psychologist, Lifecoach, Leadership Developer, Black Belt (LSS), Strategic Thinker, Talent Analyst, certified professional trainer from the U.K. and certified behavioral coach from the U.S.A.

Dr. Amit Das likes googling, reading books, writing articles & books, cooking, listening to old melodies, and counselling people to unleash their true potential to build a strong nation. He is married and blessed with a son. He would love to hear about your experience after reading his books. You can email him and share your thoughts, or you can use his services for life coaching, positive behavioural counseling, educational support, and mentoring for young, promising students pursuing their B.B.A. and M.B.A. degrees.

References

- *Personal Branding in the Digital Age: How to Become a Known Expert, Thrive and Make a Difference in a Connected World* by Francine Beleyi, Nov 2017.
- *Personal Branding - Market Yourself!: Tips To Sell Yourself And Stand Out From The Crowd* by 50minutes.com, July 2017.
- *The Essential Guide to Personal Branding: Monetise Your Expertise, Make Extraordinary Impact, and Create Financial Success* by Uju Obuekwe, July 2020.
- *Personal Branding: Master Your Digital Presence* by Felix Tim, Dec 2018.
- *Trailblazer: The Power of Business as the Greatest Platform for Change* by Marc Benoiff, Sep 2020.
- *Personal Branding 247: Everything you need to know to unearth and express your authenticity for personal success* by Andrew Chow, May 2017.
- *Your Branding Edge: How Personal Branding Can Turbocharge Your Career* by Rahna Barthelmess, Sep 2014.
- *Personal Branding: Your Personal Brand Is Your Most Valuable Asset* by Todd Gragg, Oct 2011.
- *KNOWN: The handbook for building and unleashing your personal brand in the digital age* by Mark W. Schaefer, Jan 2017.
- *Stand Out: How to Find Your Breakthrough Idea and Build a Following Around It* by Dorie Clark, Apr 2015.
- *Social Media Marketing 2019: The Power of Instagram Marketing - How to Win Followers & Influence Millions Online Using Highly Effective Personal Branding & Digital*

Networking Strategies by Robert Miller, Mar 2019.

- *From Zero to One Million Followers: Become an Influencer with Social Media Viral Growth Strategies on YouTube, Twitter, Facebook, Instagram, and the Secrets to Make Your Personal Brand known* by Jake A Clark, Jan 2020.
- *LinkedIn for Personal Branding: The Ultimate Guide* by Sandra Long, Oct 2020.
- *Reinventing You, With a New Preface: Define Your Brand, Imagine Your Future* by Dorie Clark, Oct 2017.
- *The Laws of Brand Storytelling: Win—and Keep—Your Customers' Hearts and Minds* by Ekaterina Walter and Jessica Gioglio, Nov 2018.
- *Social Media Marketing: Learn How to Become a Skilled Influencer on Facebook, Instagram, YouTube and Twitter: Top Digital Networking and Personal Branding Strategies* by Jason Miller, Nov 2020.
- *Self as Coach, Self as Leader: Developing the Best in You to Develop the Best in Others* by Pamela McLean, May 2019.
- *Branding for Millions: Business & Personal Branding* by Reece Johnson, Feb 2019.
- *Personal Branding Success Secrets: How To Use Twitter To Invent Or Reinvent Your Brand: How To Take Control Of Your Brand* by Brigitte Dilling, Aug 2021.
- *The Road to Recognition: The A-to-Z Guide to Personal Branding for Accelerating Your Professional Success in The Age of Digital Media* by Seth Price, Nov 2018.
- *Crushing It with Social Media Marketing and Personal Branding: Discover Top Entrepreneur and Influencer Viral Network and SEO Secrets for YouTube, Instagram, and Facebook Advertising* by Gary Donald, Nov 2019.
- *Social Media Marketing and Personal Branding Bible: The Practical Guide to Rapidly Growing your Business and*

Brand with Marketing and Advertising on Facebook, YouTube, Instagram and More by Gary Clyne, July 2019.

- *Social Media Marketing 2019: Your Personal Branding Guide to YouTube, Facebook Ads, Instagram, Twitter, Pinterest, SEO - Digital Advertising Secrets ... Brand for Small Businesses and Solopreneurs) by Mc Gray John, May 2019.*

- *Harness the Power of Personal Branding and Executive Presence: Elevate Your Life and Career Now! By S Renee Smith, July 2019.*

- *Personal Branding Decoded: How To Create, Grow, & Monetize Your Personal Brand Online by Gus Lopez, Jan 2019.*

- *Personal Branding Secrets: Learn How to Build your personal Brand and Become an Expert Influencer Using Social Media like Youtube, Facebook, Instagram, Pinterest by Alex Narrow, Sep 2019.*

- *Personal Branding: Why You Need to Know What Makes You unique and authentic by Lori Bumgarner, Mar 2019.*

- *Personal Branding Mastery for Entrepreneurs by Chris J Reed, Aug 2017.*

- *Instagram Influencer Marketing Adversiting 2021: Secrets on How to do Personal Branding in the Right Way and become a Top Influencer Even if you Have ... (Social Media Mastery Beginner's Guide) by Jason Miles, Mar 2021.*

- *How to Create a Personal Brand without Spending a Fortune: Affordable and Simple Ways to Promote Yourself or Business by Humphrey Snyder, Nov 2019.*

- *Personal Branding with LinkedIn: The Think Natalia Method by Dr. Natalia Wiechowski, May 2020.*

- *Getting Your Personal Brand Story Straight: ten exercises to help you get clear on the story you want to tell by Joanne*

Tombrakos, Jan 2019.

- *Build Your Personal Brand: The Definitive Guide to Soul-Based Marketing by Rachel Gogos, Dec 2018.*
- *Personal Branding Strategies The Ultimate Practical Guide to Branding And Marketing Yourself Online Through Instagram, YouTube, Facebook and Twitter ... How To Utilize Advertising on Social Media by Gary Clyne, Oct 2020.*
- *Brand Identity Breakthrough: How to Craft Your Company's Unique Story to Make Your Products Irresistible by Gregory V. Diehl and Kyle Gray, Mar 2017.*
- *Viral Personal Branding: Marketing a personal brand, building buzz and getting your dream clients by Michael Allebach, Jan 2019.*
- *HIRED! Paths to Employment In The Social Media Era by Jeff Sheehan and Alfred M Smith, Aug 2014.*
- *Social Media Marketing Mastery 2020: Build Your Brand and Become the Best Influencer Using Instagram Marketing. Discover the Top Personal Branding Strategies To Boost Your Followers (Online Business) by Oliver Alexander Martin, Mar 2020.*
- *Mindset: The New Psychology of Success, December, 2007 by Carol S. Dweck.*
- *Man's Search for Meaning, June , 2006 by Viktor E. Frankl.*
- *You Are a Badass: How to Stop Doubting Your Greatness and Start Living an Awesome Life, April, 2013 by Jen Sincero.*
- *Make Your Bed: Little Things That Can Change Your Life...And Maybe the World, April, 2017 by Admiral William H. McRaven.*
- *The Alchemist, 25th Anniversary: A Fable About Following Your Dream, April, 2014 by Paulo Coelho.*
- *Smarter Faster Better: The Transformative Power of Real*

Productivity, March, 2017 by Charles Duhigg.

- *Tuesdays with Morrie: An Old Man, a Young Man, and Life's Greatest Lesson*, 25th Anniversary Edition Kindle Edition, June, 2007 by Mitch Albom.
- *The 5 Second Rule: Transform your Life, Work, and Confidence with Everyday Courage*, February, 2017 by Mel Robbins.
- *#YOU: Build Your Personal Brand Paperback* – 15 July 2021 by Charu Sabnavis (Author).
- *Think and Grow Rich: The Landmark Bestseller Now Revised and Updated for the 21st Century (Think and Grow Rich Series)*, January, 2005 by Napoleon Hill , Arthur R. Pell.
- *Now, Discover Your Strengths: The revolutionary Gallup program that shows you how to develop your unique talents and strengths*, February, 2020 by Gallup.
- *Change Your Life: End Your Struggle & Create an Extraordinary Life in 10 Days Paperback* – 29 September 2019 by Sneh Desai (Author).
- *Change Your Life In Seven Days: The No. 1 Bestseller Paperback* – 30 May 2019 by Paul McKenna (Author).
- *Think and Grow Rich: The Landmark Bestseller Now Revised and Updated for the 21st Century (Think and Grow Rich Series)*, January, 2005 by Napoleon Hill , Arthur R. Pell.
- *Now, Discover Your Strengths: The revolutionary Gallup program that shows you how to develop your unique talents and strengths*, February, 2020 by Gallup.
- *Change Your Life: End Your Struggle & Create an Extraordinary Life in 10 Days Paperback* – 29 September 2019 by Sneh Desai (Author).
- *Change Your Life In Seven Days: The No. 1 Bestseller Paperback* – 30 May 2019 by Paul McKenna (Author).